# ADVICE

## FROM THE

# TOP

**The Expert
Guide to B2B
Marketing**

ROI

Channel
Marketing

Content

Marketing
Automation

SEO

Customer
Experience

Sales Enablement

**BMA** BUSINESS MARKETING
ASSOCIATION
Colorado

**Real-World Insights From
24 of Today's Best Marketers**

First published by Dog Ear Publishing
4010 W. 86th Street, Ste H
Indianapolis, IN 46268
www.dogearpublishing.net

ISBN: 978-145750-219-4

This paper is acid free and meets all ANSI standards for archival quality paper.
Printed in the United States of America

*"This book provides a B2B blueprint from strategy planning to marketing-mix development to measuring results. Good reference guide for marketers."*

Eduardo Conrado, Senior Vice President and Chief Marketing Officer,
Motorola Solutions, Inc.

*"This book is food for the brain of anyone who craves critical insights and proven best practices on B2B marketing from some of the finest practitioners in the business world today."*

Eileen Zicchino, Chief Marketing Officer, J.P. Morgan Treasury Services

*"Some of the best intelligence, insight and expertise on B2B marketing, and its future trends. Written by my fellow friends, what a great collaboration! Learn from them."*

Jeffrey Hayzlett, Best–Selling Author of *The Mirror Test*, Celebrity CMO, Cowboy

 BUSINESS MARKETING
ASSOCIATION
Colorado

BMA Colorado is a 13-time national Business Marketing Association
Chapter of the Year award winner.
For more information, visit us at www.bmacolorado.org.

# PREFACE AND ACKNOWLEDGMENTS

Colorado is home to the majestic Rocky Mountains and 58 "four-teeners" — mountain peaks at least 14,000 feet in altitude. Each of these mountain peaks is uniquely remarkable, with its own story and rugged profile honed over the years.

Likewise, Colorado is home to nearly 400 Business Marketing Association (BMA) members, each of whom also has his/her own unique story and experience to share. In this collaborative collection of marketing wisdom, you will hear from 24 of the best in business-to-business (B2B) marketing.

Any wise mountaineer will tell you it's critical to do your research and learn from others who have gone before you when preparing for the often perilous trek to the top. And as marketers, we are also on our own journeys, often fraught with real-world challenges and threats of a different kind. Business marketing is no less a daunting journey of trial and error, learning and growing.

Don't go it alone. Trust those who have navigated these paths before you. Learn from the collective experience of the experts represented here and experience a more enjoyable and successful journey.

This is what *Advice From the Top: The Expert Guide to B2B Marketing* is all about — taking the best of what these proven B2B professionals have to offer and sharing it with others, at whatever level of the marketing journey you're on.

This book is not necessarily designed to be read straight-through, from front to back, although it's a good read if you do. We suggest that you start with the Table of Contents and look for the chapters that address your most timely and pertinent needs and marketing challenges.

These authors can help you. They've been there and have often learned the hard way, so you don't have to. This book is designed to give you a "leg up" to the next level of your marketing career and to serve as a catalyst for new ideas and creative solutions to today's many marketing challenges. And to further guide you on your journey, each of the 24 chapters in this book includes a Case Study, because these real-world examples can be so much more helpful to your learning experience.

Are you ready for the journey? If so, you're wise to have picked up this book. It will be an important next step in equipping you for the challenges that lie ahead. You will gain valuable new perspectives from these authors and, it is our hope, that this shared experience will make you even more successful at what you do.

## Special Thanks...

This book would not have happened without the leadership, effort and personal sacrifice of many. First of all, thank you to our authors — all BMA Colorado members and marketing leaders — who have so generously and willingly shared their experience and insights with you in this book. Secondly, thanks to our many BMA board members and an amazing team of dedicated volunteers who have tirelessly worked on this project as a labor of love for hundreds of hours over many months. Specifically, thank you to Marilee Yorchak, BMA Colorado's executive director, BMA Colorado president, Carla Johnson, and editorial team members, Jay Marks, Glen Girard, Tom Kimball and Casey Demchak. Special thanks also go to Eileen Schoen, for her help with the final manuscript, and to Laurie Shields for her amazing work as this book's graphic designer and production artist. And last, but far from least, this project would never have been possible without our general editor, Marilyn Harmacek, whose passion and commitment to excellence have made this book something we can all be proud of. Thank you and congratulations all.

During my 30 years as a Business Marketing Association member, I have never witnessed a more real and tangible demonstration of BMA's mission of education and giving back to the B2B marketing community. I hope you enjoy the journey through this book as much as we've enjoyed bringing it to you.

Rich Carvill, CBC
Vice President, Education, 2010 -2011
BMA Colorado

# FOREWORD

**J**udging from how engaged I was while reading *Advice From the Top: The Expert Guide to B2B Marketing*, it is clear that the practice of business-to-business marketing and thought leadership on that subject are quite alive and quite well in Colorado.

Historically one of the largest and strongest chapters in the Business Marketing Association's 22-chapter national network, our Colorado chapter has outdone itself again — and notched another BMA system "first" — by developing this highly practical book on effective B2B marketing.

By unleashing the best thinking of 24 regional experts with corporate, agency, consulting and related backgrounds, BMA Colorado has created a soup-to-nuts handbook that should be in the library of every B2B marketer — not just in Colorado, but the rest of the U.S. and beyond.

The book is truly "advice from the top" as all contributors have 15, 20 or even 30 years or more experience practicing and mastering their areas of expertise. All 24 authors demonstrate a deep understanding of how B2B marketing is evolving. They showcase in their "advice" the latest developments and techniques in their respective spaces. No outdated legacy thinking here.

One of the remarkable features of *Advice From the Top* is that it is relevant and engaging to B2B marketers in virtually all industries and fields, and at all stages of their careers. There is material especially relevant to small- and middle-market marketers, and there is plenty of content relevant to enterprise marketers, too. It's a mother-lode-rich how-to handbook for younger marketers and a refreshing relearning, and even unlearning experience, for the most seasoned of marketers.

The book is organized logically into four sections — starting with "Building Your Strategy" and followed by "Developing Content," "Implementing Your Plan" and "Measuring Your Success." Each section contains from four to seven chapters, all adding new thinking and insight to the section theme, and all containing at least one relevant and illustrative B2B case study.

**Section 1, Building Your Strategy,** kicks off with a primer by research expert Marcy Phelps on doing customer and industry learning. Marketing executive Tom Kennedy offers a guide to creating strategic and tactical marketing plans. Agency principal Brett Schklar describes how to build buyer personas to achieve better sales-marketing integration. Sales consultant Orlin Camerlo discusses how to boost your pipeline through integrated teleprospecting. CMO Lisa Miller describes how to create a successful customer-retention plan. Business-school professor Charles Patti shares his thinking on successfully managing the customer experience. And business-writing expert Larry Brummond discusses five critical success factors for entrepreneurs.

**Section 2, Developing Content,** begins with agency executive Sam Eidson sharing a roadmap for conversion-driven marketing based on targeting information offers to B2B buyers. Business-writing expert Casey Demchak follows with tips on mastering persuasive business-writing techniques. CMO Marian Robinson discusses the importance of value-based content. Communications consultant Carla Johnson, 2010-2011 president of BMA Colorado, weighs in on telling your company story from the inside out. Communications expert Tom Schippert discusses ten steps to integrating social media. And professors Maria van Dressel and Charles Patti review literalism vs. symbolism in B2B advertising.

**Section 3, Implementing Your Plan,** gets under way with agency exec and channel-marketing expert Scott Gillum discussing how to improve partner relationships. Marketing consultant Laurie Lavelle shares tips on ensuring marketing success through strategic execution. Agency exec and social-media expert Yann Ropars describes how to use PR 2.0 to increase your brand's competitive edge. IT and Web-design expert Michael Ward discusses inbound lead generation and marketing automation strategies. High-tech marketer Kevin Thomas shares his experience integrating sales and marketing operations. Agency execs Cheryl Ader Smith and Lisa Haldeman follow with tips on best practices in sales enablement. Finally, agency exec Melanie Hughes Goetz discusses the magic, mystery and marketing psychology behind masterful B2B advertising.

**Section 4, Measuring Your Success,** launches with a review by corporate marketer Byron O'Dell of "ROI 101" and the importance of building measurement into today's marketing programs. Precision-marketing experts Sandra Zoratti and Lee Gallagher follow with a primer on maximizing return on marketing investment (ROMI). Direct-marketing experts David Ariss and Susan Fantle discuss proven direct marketing demand generation techniques. And marketing and event-management consultant Barry Siedenstat wraps up both the section and the book with advice on how to use voice-of-customer (VOC) data to measure event success.

In a world awash with marketing-management books, *Advice From the Top* stands out as a most useful addition. BMA Colorado has done business marketers worldwide a huge service by marshalling the diverse voices and thinking of so many marketing experts — from leading academics to in-the-trenches corporate marketers to senior agency executives and seasoned consultants. It is a book to read, share, re-read, fill with Post-it® notes, scribble on, photocopy, scan, Tweet and blog about, read aloud to others, share with clients and staff, and sleep on.

For years, I have asked all employees in my firm to read a mainstay stable of marketing books, including classics by Al Ries, Don and Heidi Schultz, Phil Kotler, Joe Pine and Jim Gilmore, Sergio Zyman and others. In *Advice From the Top: The Expert Guide to B2B Marketing*, I have come across another excellent book to add to that required reading list. And add it I will, as soon as I get my hands on 100 copies!


Gary Slack
National Chairman, 2009-2011, Business Marketing Association
Chairman and Chief Experience Officer, Slack + Company

# BUILDING YOUR STRATEGY

1 | From Zero to Strategy: Mining the Info-Sphere for
Marketing Insights – **Marcy Phelps** ...................................................3

2 | How to Develop Winning Marketing Plans –
**Tom Kennedy** .........................................................................13

3 | The Power of Who: Creating a Fully Integrated
Marketing Program – **Brett A. Schklar** .........................................25

4 | Expand Your Pipeline Through Integrated Teleprospecting –
**Orlin Camerlo** .......................................................................35

5 | Keys to Creating a Successful Customer-Retention Plan –
**Lisa A. Miller** .........................................................................41

6 | Successfully Managing the Customer Experience –
**Dr. Charles H. Patti** ................................................................47

7 | Five Critical Success Factors for Entrepreneurs –
**Larry Brummond** ...................................................................57

# DEVELOPING CONTENT

8 | A Roadmap for Conversion-Driven Marketing –
**Sam Eidson** ...........................................................................69

9 | Mastering Persuasive B2B Sales Writing Techniques –
**Casey Demchak** .....................................................................77

10 | Why Value-Based Content Is King –
**Marian Robinson** ...................................................................87

11 | Telling Your Company Story From the Inside Out –
**Carla Johnson** ........................................................................95

12 | Ten Steps to Integrating Social Media –
**Tom Schippert** ...................................................................... 103

13 | Just Give Me the Facts: Literalism vs. Symbolism in B2B Advertising –
**Dr. Maria van Dessel** and **Dr. Charles H. Patti** ........................ 111

# IMPLEMENTING YOUR PLAN

14 | Improving Partner Relationships in Today's
Competitive Landscape – **Scott Gillum**.......................................123

15 | Ensuring Marketing Success Through Strategic Execution –
**Laurie Lavelle** .................................................................................129

16 | Using PR 2.0 to Increase Your Brand's Competitive Edge –
**Yann Ropars**....................................................................................135

17 | Inbound Lead Generation and Marketing
Automation Strategies – **Michael Ward**....................................143

18 | Marketing and Sales — Friends or Foes? –
**Kevin Thomas** ................................................................................151

19 | Best Practices for Sales Enablement –
**Cheryl A. Smith** and **Lisa Haldeman** ....................................157

20 | Inside Mirror Marketing Psychology –
**Melanie Hughes Goetz** ................................................................165

# MEASURING SUCCESS

21 | Driving ROI Into Today's Marketing Programs –
**Byron O'Dell** ..................................................................................175

22 | Maximizing Return on Marketing Investment (ROMI) –
**Sandra Zoratti** and **Lee Gallagher** ..........................................183

23 | Proven Direct Marketing Demand Generation Techniques –
**David Ariss** and **Susan Fantle** ...................................................193

24 | Using Voice of the Customer (VOC) to Measure Event Success –
**Barry Seidenstadt**..........................................................................201

# BUILDING YOUR STRATEGY

ADVICE FROM THE TOP

# 1 | From Zero to Strategy
## Mining the Info-Sphere for Market Insights

Marcy Phelps

T he most effective business-to-business (B2B) marketing decisions are informed decisions. The marketplace is too competitive and the cost of doing business too high to make decisions about marketing strategy without a clear understanding of your market — your buyers, your competitors, and the environment in which you and they operate. Whether launching a new product, looking for market opportunities or exploring ways to be more competitive, your company's marketing strategy depends on your knowledge about the market. You'll need to discover whether it's an open or saturated market, determine your competitive advantage and decide the best way to reach your market. These insights can be found through an organized study of the market, which generally starts by asking several questions.

| Competition | Buyers | Industry |
|---|---|---|
| Who are our direct and indirect competitors? | Who are our potential customers? | What is the size of the market? |
| What is their share of the market? | What are their demographics? (Number of companies, company size, etc.) | What is the outlook for this market? Is it expected to shrink, expand or remain stable? |
| How do they position themselves in the marketplace? | What motivates them to buy these types of products/services? | How is the industry segmented? |
| What products/services do they offer? | Where do they go to learn about these types of products/services? | Who are the market leaders? |
| How do they differentiate their products/services? | What frustrates them about the buying process? | What trends and issues affect this industry (social, cultural, financial, demographic, political)? |
| How do they price their products/services? | Do they consider our products/ services essential or "nice to have"? | What technology innovations will affect this industry? |
| What marketing channels do they use? | What do they expect from these products/services? | What legislation/regulations affect this industry? |
| What are their strengths and weaknesses? | What price are they willing to pay? | What risks/challenges does this industry face? |

There's no shortage of information in the digital age. You can run a Google search, download a market research report, conduct focus groups and put together a survey — all with the click of a mouse. However, Web searching, interviews, surveys and packaged reports merely provide the pieces to the puzzle. The best market studies — the ones that offer the most strategic insights to B2B companies — have two characteristics in common.

- They use information that has been gathered in a variety of ways, including Web-based and human sources. One-on-one conversations, usually conducted by phone with industry experts, customers and even your competitors, can fill in the gaps for what you've found on the Web.
- They include analysis through every step of the process. There's more to research than just gathering information. Analysis helps connect the dots, add insights and answer the questions you never thought to ask.

This chapter takes you through a three-step process for gaining an understanding of B2B markets. It involves getting ready for research, gathering intelligence and turning the findings into strategic knowledge. It's a framework that can be used by any B2B marketer, regardless of industry, type of business or marketing goals.

## Step 1. Getting Ready for Research

The more prepared you are for your market study, the better the results. To set up an effective research strategy, it's best to start by answering several important questions.

- What's the purpose of this research?
- Who needs the research?
- What's being done with it?
- What do you already know?
- What do you still need to know?
- If it can't be found, what information would be good enough?
- What's the budget and timeframe?

Your goal is to list and prioritize key intelligence questions, which provide the focus for research and facilitate analysis during the next two steps. Knowing how the research will be used assures that the right information will be provided in the most useful format. If the results will ultimately be used in a presentation, you might summarize results in a few PowerPoint slides. If you're presenting statistics, think about charts, tables or graphs to convey your key points.

Pull together any previously gathered information to avoid duplication in the research. This information is also a great source of important clues that can be used for your research, including key terms, a breakdown of subtopics or leads to new sources. Keep an open mind during this brainstorming session: think creatively and explore all possibilities. Your original questions may not be the only path to the answers you need.

Because you really can't be sure you'll find exactly what you're looking for, think about alternatives. In case you can't find ten-year local-level economic projections, will five-year estimates make a good substitute? If the competition won't provide prices, will it help to get an idea of their pricing models?

Take what you've learned during this brainstorming and map out your research strategy. Determine the best sources based on your budget, timeframe and key questions. Then, divide the tasks and outline appropriate checkpoints for evaluating the process and results.

When you're gathering and analyzing market intelligence, it's important to understand that there's no such thing as "free information." Think about the value of your time the next time you're considering whether to spend three hours gathering industry data vs. purchasing a $200 packaged report that contains just about everything you need.

Once you've prepared for your research, it's time to dive into the "info-sphere," the vast collection of electronic and human sources available today.

## Step 2. Mining the Info-Sphere for Market Intelligence

You want to start your search online even if your research plan includes telephone interviews, surveys or other types of research. Web searching will help you identify and learn about the people you're targeting, and the background information that you gather from online sources will help you ask more intelligent questions.

### Cast a Wide Net

Begin with a general purpose search engine such as Google, using broad terms and phrases. The purpose here is to scan the information environment — definitions, keywords, subtopics and leads to sources — and prepare for the rest of the research. Don't get too targeted at this point or you might miss something valuable. Search for your industry name combined with keywords such as *trends, forecasts* or *outlook*. Add *market research* to the mix to find packaged reports and news articles about these reports. Press releases from market research providers often contain useful statistics about market size, segments or competition — information you can gather without purchasing the reports. Scan sources that will help you identify the big players in the industry, your competitors' customers, and other key pieces of information about your market. Try this same search in one or two other search engines since each one will return different results.

If you find that your search results aren't really relevant or there are too many to scan, go to the advanced search page. Try narrowing your search by date or location. Another trick is to limit by file type: statistics can frequently be found in spreadsheets; annual reports are usually in PDF; and executives often post PowerPoint slides.

Don't forget to check the websites of national and local organizations such as chambers of commerce, economic development groups and trade associations. Many offer demographics, market statistics, industry information or lists of top companies. If you don't find what you need, pick up the phone and call their executive directors or other leaders. If they don't have the information, it's likely they will know who does. Check committee rosters and membership directories for contacts that can be used during the phone research phase.

Take what you've learned and move on to searching news and trade journals, including articles, opinion pieces and other content. This can be done by going directly to the websites of specific sources or through news aggregators — sites that gather content from a variety of sources. Depending on your budget and timeframe, several fee-based sources, such as Dow Jones Factiva (www.factiva.com) and Dialog (www.dialog.com), offer special features that allow you to quickly mine news content from their vast collections of business resources.

News comes in all shapes and sizes, so don't forget the alternative press, journalist blogs and news in audio and video formats. Local news outlets are especially useful for learning about a particular geographic place, and they provide in-depth coverage of their home-grown companies and industries. Again, cast a wide net and follow all leads. Make note of the names of people writing the articles and the people about whom they're writing. It will help you identify and learn about possible targets for your telephone research, or people to call for leads to additional resources.

**Finding Your Focus**
After you've done this general research, it's time for sources that are more targeted toward your industry and your specific list of questions.

Before you begin, gather and review your findings to discover your information gaps. Do you still need company-related information? Are you missing a few industry projections? This review will help you select the right resources and narrow your focus. If you still need some demographics, business statistics or industry data, try the U.S. Census Bureau (www.census.gov), Bureau of Economic Analysis (www.bea.gov) or the Bureau of Labor Statistics (www.bls.gov). For details about your competitors, go to Hoover's (www.hoovers.com) or other company directories. If you still need market forecasts or industry trends, packaged market research or industry reports might be the best approach.

Don't neglect social media. B2B companies are blogging and tweeting, and their current and past employees are connecting on LinkedIn and Facebook. Search social networking profiles, groups, comments, recommendations, discussions and other social-Web hot spots for information about companies, buyers and industry experts.

**Let's Chat**
The next phase of your research is gathering information from human sources. Unlike online research, where you can always redo your search, there are no second chances with telephone interviews so you want to approach these very carefully. Whether you're looking for insights from experts in the field — potential, current and past customers, or people who work or have worked for the competition — some basic rules apply to conducting telephone research.

- **Be prepared.** Make sure you know your topic well enough to ask intelligent questions and understand the answers. Arm yourself with lots of possible contacts. The more you have, the easier it will be to complete the required number of interviews.
- **Respect their time.** These people are taking time out of their busy schedules to talk with you. Set and stick to a time limit. Keep your calls to no more than 30-40 minutes.
- **Consider confidentiality.** Decide ahead of time what information you want to divulge about your research. Consider the fact that making calls and asking questions could very possibly alert your competition.
- **Be ethical.** Never lie or misrepresent yourself. If you wish to remain anonymous, consider hiring a third party.
- **Be a giver.** Offer something in return for someone's time and expertise. A short, top-level executive summary of your findings will often persuade people to share what they know.

When you have everything you need to answer your key questions, you can take the final step toward understanding your market.

## Step 3. Turning Research Into Strategic Knowledge

Information by itself is meaningless. Insights emerge only after analysis. The following tips will add insights and help you discover what the gathered information means to your company's strategy.

- Look for patterns and connections in the information.
- Read each piece of information within the context of what else you know. Always ask what it means for your market strategy.
- Pull out what's most useful based on your market study's purpose and key questions.
- Summarize the vital points that answer the questions or help complete the profile of your market.
- Create charts, tables and graphs to highlight major concepts and facilitate insights.
- More is not always better. Package results with just the right amount of information to support the decision-making process.

It should be noted that strategic research is not a one-time event. It is a process that takes place over time, providing an early-warning system for sudden changes that can and do occur in B2B markets. Set up RSS feeds or Google alerts for monitoring the information landscape on an ongoing basis. Update your market knowledge by annually conducting online and telephone research.

This three-step intelligence process is the foundation for critical, information-based decisions about B2B marketing strategy. The insights gained from the analysis of your customers, competitors and industry will make it possible to more accurately assess market and product potential, minimize risk and improve long-term planning.


## CASE STUDY
### Reefer Madness: A Study of the Refrigerated Trucking Market

**The Challenge.** A technology company was expanding its product line and planned to target the refrigerated trucking market, including companies with over-the-road trucks and those carrying road-to-rail containers — also known as reefer trucks. The company needed information about this new market before beginning its strategic planning.

**The Client.** The company produces mobile asset management software and hardware that tracks refrigerated trucks and containers, and manages the temperature and other environmental controls.

**The Journey.** The marketing team gathered press releases, articles and other information from the Web and purchased two market research reports. While these sources provided interesting nuggets, the team was left with several unanswered questions.

**The Discovery.** Phelps Research was contacted by Don, the firm's head of marketing and a former Phelps client.

**The Solution.** Don wanted to know about his competition and their products and services. He was unsure about who made the buying decisions and what features were important to them. Phelps Research suggested he include industry information in the search because this would help analyze the market more effectively. Based on preliminary research, the results of the marketing team's research, and the information gathered from several conversations with Don, Phelps decided to utilize a combination of sources, including free and fee-based online resources and one-on-one telephone interviews. Don approved the project scope as outlined.

- Research mobile asset management industry trends, issues and outlook.
- Research competitive environment.
  - Identify mobile asset management companies targeting the refrigerated trucking market.
  - Compile profiles on top 10 competing companies (by annual sales):
    - Products/services
    - Positioning
    - Marketing channels
    - Strengths/weaknesses
    - Conduct buyer research
- Identify potential customers
- Conduct ten to twelve 30-minute interviews with potential customers.
  - Who is the ultimate buyer in the company?
  - What technology are they currently using?
  - How many units would they potentially need?
  - What are they looking for in this type of product?
  - What's missing in the current offerings?

**The Implementation.** The first step was to gather background information on the mobile asset monitoring industry by researching organizations, professional publications and major players in the refrigerated trucking market. This information would be the foundation for more in-depth online research and for the telephone interviews. This process included general searching in Google, Biznar (www.Biznar.com) and Carrot2 (search.carrot2.org), combining keywords such as *mobile, asset, management* and *tracking* with *trends, outlook, forecast, outlook* and *market research*. It uncovered several press releases about the company's competitors, their product lines and their marketing strategy. Specialized searching discovered the websites of *Commercial Carrier Journal* (www.ccjdigital.com), *Refrigerated Transporter* (www.refrigeratedtrans.com) and *Telematics Journal* (www.telematicsjournal.com). These provided industry and competitor information from recent articles and lists of links to additional online resources.

Mining professional online databases, including Dialog and Dow Jones Factiva, provided relevant articles, strengths/weaknesses/opportunities/threats (SWOT) analyses and other company-related information. These sources led to a recent market study on trailer monitoring systems and services, and helped expand the list of experts and competitors. Searching company directories, such as Hoover's (www.hoovers.com), ThomasNet (www.thomasnet.com) and those offered in Dialog, helped identify contacts for telephone research.

At this point, Phelps Research was ready to start the second phase of the project: buyer research. All the information was sent to the phone researcher along with a list of the key questions outlined in the research agreement. While the phone researcher worked on the interviews, Phelps Research completed the competitor profiles, using a table format for easy comparisons.

| Company | Annual Sales ($ million) Services | Products/ Positioning | Channels | Strengths/ Weaknesses | Notes |
|---|---|---|---|---|---|
| Company 1 Web: Address: Phone: | | | | | |
| | | | | | |
| | | | | | |

Sources used for the profiles included Hoover's, Dow Jones Factiva, the websites of the companies, and Morningstar Document Research (documentresearch.morningstar.com), a specialized database for extracting information from SEC filings. Topix (www.topix.com) and the advanced search page for Google News (news.google.com) were used, for private companies, to search the news from, or about, the region in which they were headquartered.

The final report included several elements:
- Cover letter with overview of project, including key questions, approach to the research and a concise, top-level summary of the findings
- Table of contents
- Executive summary
- Charts and graphs with industry statistics
- Table with buyer interview responses organized by question
- Competitor profiles/matrix
- Appendix with all supporting documents, including full-text articles and reports, plus interview summaries

**The Results.** Based on the report, company executives decided to move ahead with plans to enter the refrigerated trucking market. Although the interviews covered a small sample of prospects in this market, they showed that Don's company's products offered the features most desired by the interview subjects. The company also decided to aggressively market its support services, since the interviews indicated that service was a high priority when making this sort of investment. To stay current, Don asked for bi-monthly updates on industry, buyer and competitor news. He and his team were also ready to explore several other target markets for their mobile asset management hardware, software and services.

**Marcy Phelps** is the founder and principal of Phelps Research, a company that helps its clients find and understand strategic business information. Marcy has been a member of the Colorado chapter of the Business Marketing Association since 2002 and served on the board of directors as secretary from 2006-2008. She regularly writes and speaks on business and market intelligence and is the author of *Research on Main Street: Using the Web to Find Local Business and Market Information*.

# 2 | How To Develop Winning Marketing Plans

Tom Kennedy

**D**espite its frequent use, this quote remains relevant to the B2B world and to the discipline of marketing, in particular. Planning is the first step towards ensuring the best possible chance of a business

> *"Failing to plan is planning to fail"* cautions the well-worn organizational nugget.

success, especially for small and mid-size businesses (SMB) seeking to create sustainable value in their respective marketplaces.

Marketing plans are important for businesses of any size seeking to create value for customers and shareholders. Too often though, SMBs — those businesses the Yankee Group characterizes as containing fewer than 500 employees[1] — are the ones who either neglect the process altogether or fail to follow through on the execution side.

The causes for these shortcomings are many. B2B-focused SMB marketers face challenges essentially unknown to their large-company counterparts, including inferior name recognition, insufficient financial resources, elongated sales cycles, multiple personalities and "touches" along the buying cycle, and the marketing "idea of the day" rendered by senior management or well-meaning co-workers.

As the head of an SMB's marketing organization, it is incumbent upon this role to overcome these disadvantages while breathing life into the business plan. The critical action is establishing a strategic marketing program with clear descriptions of the company, what it does, its target markets and the competitive landscape. Then, with the strategic roadmap in hand, the lead marketer must create and drive the execution of a tight tactical marketing plan. Both types of marketing plans — strategic and tactical — are outlined in this chapter.

# Strategic Marketing Plans

So, what is a strategic marketing plan? How is it different from a business plan or corporate strategy document?

In general terms, a strategic marketing plan is a document that describes the current situation with regard to your customers, your competitors and the attributes of your product or service. As a blueprint for action, highlighting your company's approach all of the elements needed to create a consistently effective value exchange between your company and your target markets, the strategic document typically covers a three- to five-year period and is updated as markets and economic conditions change.

The core items are your business mission, vision, tag line, graphical brand identity, market research, market segmentation, strengths-weaknesses-opportunities-threats (SWOT) analysis and competitive intelligence. Without this roadmap, it is difficult to align a small or medium-size business' finite set of resources behind a common business purpose, let alone have consistent messaging or a clear focus on target audiences.

## Key Steps to Creating a Strategic Marketing Plan

**1. Collect the data from your business plan.** Extract as much pertinent information from the business plan as possible to answer the following questions:
- Who are we and what's our brand?
  - Company description, mission, vision
  - Company brand components, including tag line
- What are we selling?
- Who is our target market (industry vertical) and to whom (buyer persona) in the target market are we selling?
- What are the pain points/needs experienced by our target audiences? Can we map our product's benefits to those pain points?
- What are our product's unique selling propositions? What features make us different?
- What unique core competencies or skill sets do we possess that make us good at making this product and delivering this value proposition on a repeatable basis?
- What gives us a competitive advantage in delivering this value?

**2. Collect the data from your customers.** The collective voice of your customers should drive some of the data points described above.

Get to know them better by asking them directly or by listening to them speak out in various online channels, such as industry blogs or social media forums. Once you're better acquainted, it is essential to explicitly connect the dots between customers' needs and company benefits. Without this, nothing else matters.

For SMBs with a little bit of an operating history, a practical way to start the customer conversation process is to employ a satisfaction survey. Doing so will help you discover your fans as well as any unsatisfied clients. Turn your "fans" into customer case studies. Meanwhile, make it a priority to effectively communicate and repair relationships with unsatisfied customers.

Inevitably, communicating directly with customers and prospects will also lead you to gaps between their needs and what your company can actually deliver. Either way, your company will have a business decision to make in terms of refining its target market or refining its product to better serve a particular target market. A laser-like focus on tightly defined target markets is often a make-or-break factor for startups and SMBs. Simply stated, smaller organizations do not have the resources to be all things to all people. The marketing leader should play a pivotal role in keeping the organization on track.

**3. Zero in on target markets.** The target markets defined in the strategic plan should be supported by research, whether it be conducted directly (primary research) or through professional resources. The research should answer:

- What is the size of this market?
  - · Number of customers
  - · Dollars spent annually
- Do the features and benefits of our product adequately match the needs of a particular vertical market?
- How is demand for our product or service measured?
- Who else is competing in this market? Is it a fragmented or consolidated market?
- How does our offer compare to the marketplace alternatives (price-features comparison)?

After gathering data in this area, the organization again has a business decision to make: Does it make economic sense to either enter or stay in this market? If repeatable value can be delivered at acceptable profit margins to this market, then the answer is yes and this target should remain in your plan.

At this stage it is also important to define the competition and their respective positions in the marketplace. Many approach this issue via their SWOT analysis. What are each competitor's strengths and weaknesses? What are the barriers to entry into this market? Can we achieve a sustainable edge?

**4. Zero in on the targets within the target markets.** After concluding which target markets are the best fit with the products or services offered by your company, it is essential to look at the target-within-the-target. This is critical for B2B companies because of the innate differences in the selling cycle compared to the business-to-consumer (B2C) selling cycle. As noted by social media marketing expert Chris Brogan, B2B features a "continuous touch" and lengthy relationship building at a number of organizational levels. "The biggest discernible difference in business communications between those two groups (B2B and B2C) is the justification of purchases."[2]

This underscores the importance of relationship-building with the solution finders (problem-solving initiators), users, influencers and decision makers at your target companies. Again, it is essential for the B2B marketer to understand the various organizational personas or "titles" that make up the buying cycle at a prospect organization, including:

- Who is your "initiator persona" — the staff person who performs the front-end research into solving a pain point for his or her organization?
- Who are the end-users of the product or service?
- Who are the influencers and decision makers involved in the target customer's buying process?

Brief "personas" should be developed for each role, detailing demographic features, the things each care most about, and the places they go for industry intelligence and opinions from peers. Looking ahead to the tactical marketing plan, you will need to evaluate the sales and marketing required to nurture and move the right organizational people toward a favorable buying decision.

The critical component upon completing the strategic marketing plan is to review with, and get final buy-in from, the senior team. Expect alterations along the way, but know that your ability to connect the dots between the marketing plan and the business plan will go a long way toward corner-office sponsorship. Down the road, the "sponsored" plan should also serve to eliminate misunderstandings or ambiguities between all internal stakeholders.

## Tactical Marketing Plans

Tactical marketing plans spell out the line items that mobilize the concepts highlighted at the strategic level and what you expect to spend on this mobilization. Often they are prepared or revised on a quarterly basis and help put the teeth into a marketing program.

### Key Steps to Creating a Tactical Marketing Plan

**1. Use your strategic plan as baseline.** Drawing from your strategic plan (remembering that it has sponsorship at the highest levels), begin thinking about the tactics that will support the achievement of the strategic goals. A key, especially for SMB B2B companies, is to keep the tactical marketing plan focused. Resist the temptation to create a marketing mix that taps every possible medium or mechanism to find potential customers. Be prepared to test certain activities, monitor progress and revise your plan accordingly.

**2. Determine the marketing mix.** Core to determining the marketing mix is the target customer personas developed in your strategic plan. Understanding their basic demographic make-up, their likes, dislikes and hot-button issues should help this process. Ask:

- What trade shows and conferences do they attend?
- Where do they go online for information?
- What trade publications do they read?
- Are there associations that represent a vast majority of your target audience?

In the spirit of "fishing where the fish are," answering these questions drives up the likelihood that the dollars spent on sales and marketing will result in qualified leads and the growth of a profitable customer base.

**3. Back your plan with the right financial data.** A good offense should be complemented by a good defense. The ability to defend your marketing tactics — such as exhibiting at a particular trade show or advertising on a specific industry website portal — is strengthened with return on investment (ROI) data. Historically, this has been a daunting task for marketers because of the challenges faced in capturing data on incremental sales. The good news, however, is that arriving at ROI has been made simpler by the trend toward trackable online tactics such as search engine advertising and the growing popularity of sophisticated tracking tools such as Salesforce.com. The hurdle for many is that there are still some nebulous assumptions that go into determining expected ROI for pure branding tactics (such as logo development) or traditional lead-and-branding tactics (such as trade shows). Nonetheless, the effort to establish ROI expectations remains essential.

**4. Tie actions to rational, responsible, expected measurements.** Tactical action plans should highlight the strategic reasoning for pursuing the tactic; expected budget amounts and expected ROI; due dates; measurement standards; and, responsible parties. In other words, you need to summarize:

- What are we doing?
- Why are we doing it? (Drive demand in a particular segment or to build brand?)
- What will it cost? What is our expected ROI?
- What will we measure?
- Who is responsible?
- When is it due?

**5. Formalize the budget.** Upon completing your marketing-mix project task list, a budget for the period should be formalized and internally approved. Larger organizations often look at marketing budgets from a year-over-year percentage increase (or decrease) standpoint. Other firms — both large and small — opt to analyze the marketing budget as a percentage of expected revenue in any given year. They will zero in on industry standards and try to place themselves in the same *percentage-of-sales* comfort zone. Still others will look at the budget from a top-down perspective, focusing on sales targets for the year and estimating a percentage of revenue that will come from new leads. This approach also looks at cost-per-lead and typical closing ratios to help create a more concrete pathway to a demand generation-centric marketing budget.

No matter the methodology, challenging economic times call for a marketing budget that can be defended with ROI and realistic assumptions.

**6. Review and revise.** Consistently reviewing and revising your tactical approach to marketing is also a requirement. As mentioned above, markets and economic conditions are in a constant state of change. Failing to track results and review and refine your tactics can be a recipe for disaster. Small-business experts like Duct Tape Marketing's John Jantsch, recommend that marketing plans be reviewed and tweaked every six weeks or so. "The main point is that you commit to a schedule so that your plan never has a chance to decay," says Jantsch.[3]

## Summary

Clearly, marketing plans should be designed with actions in mind — bringing to life the very essence of the business mission. They should prescribe proactive plans to grow your brand and to create demand generation (and sales) within profitable target markets.

Small and mid-size B2B companies are well served maintaining a narrow strategic focus, especially in the early stages of the business, and to align their limited financial, human and marketing resources behind a few tightly defined target market segments. The marketer's challenge is to successfully navigate the company through inferior name recognition in the marketplace, insufficient financial resources, long sales cycles, multiple personalities along the buying cycle, and the marketing "idea du jour." Strategic and tactical marketing planning, done well, help cut through the clutter and keep the organization on task with clear visibility toward business goals.

At the end of the day, marketers are evaluated based on their ability to leverage resources — including time, budget dollars and the supply chain — to advance the vision of the company and to create shareholder value. The disciplined leadership of marketing, whether it rides on the shoulders of the person holding the title of chief marketing officer or marketing manager, starts with proper planning. After all, nobody plans to fail.

## CASE STUDY
## Financial Services Software Vendor

**The Client.** The client is a small independent software vendor. Its core software offering is an accounting system developed for vertical markets in the financial services industry. The system is highly customizable and features a rich set of capabilities covering account setups, management, billing and accounts receivable. The product is available both as an enterprise license and as a Web-based offering.

**The Challenge.** The company is led by an entrepreneur who is both a technical expert in software development and well-versed in the nuances of the financial services industry. In fact, the company's software package has evolved into one of the most robust and feature-rich in the industry because of the president's persistent trouble-shooting and product revisions on behalf of individual customers. As the organization, with its limited resources, focused on the technical perfection of the product, a number of significant customer brand disconnects and product implementation issues emerged. In addition, sales and marketing activities were unfocused and unmeasured. As a result, the company struggled to increase year-over-year sales and endured high costs per lead. It took on customers requiring high-touch but yielding low profit margins and a high proportion of non-recurring revenue from one-time license sales vs. recurring revenue from the Web-based offering.

**The Journey.** In 2005, the company hired a sales/marketing manager to implement the tactical activities already in place. Unfortunately, this failed to have an overall impact on branding and sales because the situation still lacked leadership, a formal marketing plan and alignment with sales and marketing tactics. New sales remained flat and at less-than-desirable profit margins.

**The Solution.** The first step taken by the new marketing director, brought on board in mid-2006, was a brief but effective marketing audit. This snapshot was accomplished by reviewing the business plan and the marketing mix, and by conducting interviews with senior management, sales staff and customers. In aggregate, this audit highlighted the company's struggles:
- Branding inconsistencies
- Marketplace visibility
- Prospect attraction in profitable vertical markets
- Competing sales and marketing efforts (separate websites, collateral items)
- High costs per lead compared to industry averages due to largely unmanaged Internet marketing campaigns
- Poor pay-per-click performance
  - Exorbitant overall cost per click
  - Short-tail keywords yielding unqualified clicks
  - Google ads carrying different messaging and branding than ads on a popular business software portal
- Little or no organic search visibility

· Website pages not optimized with keywords, meta tags
· Small amount of incoming backlinks
· Spotty trade show participation and performance
· Lack of strategic focus (right vertical markets)
· Poorly planned lead generation activities pre-event, during event, and post-event
· Very long sales cycles
• Dysfunctional internal communication system

Against this backdrop, a strategic marketing plan was developed and included consistent brand and product identities; clear identification of target markets; a competitive landscape review and a gap analysis related to the product; and, target customer pain points. This was directly aligned with the company's business plan — now revised as a result of the marketing plan exercise — and organization-wide objectives, including the goal to sell more Web-based service packages.

A key element of the strategic plan was the development of customer personas for each area of responsibility represented in the typical buying cycle: the IT manager (solutions initiator); the operations manager (influencer); and the vice president of business development (decision maker). Gaining insights into each of these personas was accomplished over a three-week period via an online customer survey and by interviewing the sales director.

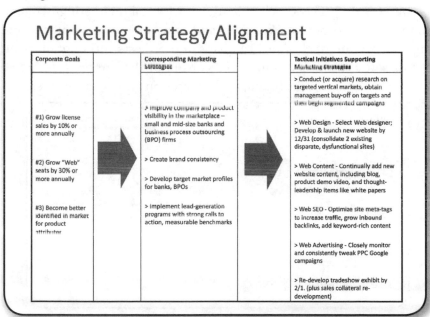

## Marketing Strategy Alignment

| Corporate Goals | Corresponding Marketing Strategies | Tactical Initiatives Supporting Marketing Strategies |
|---|---|---|
| #1) Grow license sales by 10% or more annually | > Improve company and product visibility in the marketplace – small and mid-size banks and business process outsourcing (BPO) firms | > Conduct (or acquire) research on targeted vertical markets, obtain management buy-off on targets and then begin segmented campaigns |
| #2) Grow "Web" seats by 30% or more annually | > Create brand consistency<br><br>> Develop target market profiles for banks, BPOs | > Web Design - Select Web designer; Develop & launch new website by 12/31 (consolidate 2 existing disparate, dysfunctional sites)<br><br>> Web Content - Continually add new website content, including blog, product demo video, and thought-leadership items like white papers |
| #3) Become better identified in market for product attributes | > Implement lead-generation programs with strong calls to action, measurable benchmarks | > Web SEO - Optimize site meta-tags to increase traffic, grow inbound backlinks, add keyword-rich content<br><br>> Web Advertising - Closely monitor and consistently tweak PPC Google campaigns<br><br>> Re-develop tradeshow exhibit by 2/1. (plus sales collateral re-development) |

A tactical plan — internally branded as a "Jump Start" program — was developed to bump up lead activity being managed by the sales team. The tactical plan was created concurrently with a new business plan, also driven by the new marketing director. Besides lead-generation activities, the tactical plan included rebranding activities related to the website. Specifically, two different websites — one featuring the license version of the software and one featuring the Web-based version — were consolidated over a six-month period and redesigned with a look and feel more in line with the brand vision articulated by the company president. Despite challenges with the Web host and a non-existent content management system, content and meta tags were optimized through a collaborative effort between marketing and IT resources.

During a three-week period, the new marketing leader restructured paid advertising programs at Google, Yahoo and an online software catalog in favor of longer-tail keywords, more targeted messaging and campaign structures, strategic time-of-day scheduling, and daily cost ceilings. Over the next several months, content marketing efforts were also initiated, including a best-practices white paper available via the website in exchange for minimal contact information. Hard- and soft-copy sales collateral used in the lead nurturing process were also re-developed and redesigned, all using in-house publishing competencies because of a reluctance to expand the budget.

**The Results.** The development of a formal marketing strategy, aligned with corporate objectives, and subsequent development and implementation of clear tactical plans and projects, although difficult at times due to the entrepreneurial culture of the company, have had a positive impact on the brand, lead generation and sales conversions.

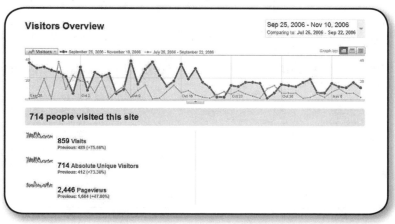

During the first six months, the company saw an increase in Web traffic as the result of adjustments made to the company's SEO and paid advertising strategies. As an example, Web analytics tracked for the seven weeks saw a 75 percent uptick in site visitors compared to the previous eight weeks. Since that time of measurement, the company has experienced peaks and valleys in its search engine marketing, but has benefited by its overall settlement as a page-one, top-six appearance on Google in the latest tracking report before publication .

From a branding standpoint, the company now possesses a single website and consistent sales collateral related to vertical market data sheets, product and company overview sheets, and customer case studies. As a result of these deliverables, plus support for sales calling scripts and e-mail messaging, the company's overall messaging to customers has been more consistent in the past two years than it was fours years ago. In addition, sales people have done a better job of setting expectations with clients. A small customer survey conducted in September 2010 showed that 75 percent of respondents indicated that the application had delivered on its promise and performed in line with expectations. An April 2007 survey indicated quite the opposite with 80 percent of respondents saying the application had not measured up to the pre-sale expectations.

Since implementing formal marketing programs — in particular, better targeting and targeted messaging — the company has seen an improvement in lead quality, cost-per-lead and total sales. Leads considered high quality — measured as leads converted to one-on-one live demonstrations of the product — increased 24 percent for the six months ended June 30, 2007 versus the same period in 2006. Total leads converted to sales improved from eight percent for the six months ended June 30, 2006 to 13 percent for the same period a year later, another indicator that leads generated were of overall better quality.

| | 6 mos. ended 6/30/2006 | 6 mos. ended 6/30/2007 |
|---|---|---|
| Total Leads | 153 | 178 |
| Leads Considered "Highly Qualified" | 42 | 52 |
| Total Leads Converted to Sales | 12 | 23 |
| % of Highly qualified leads | 27% | 29% |
| % of Leads Converted to Sales | 8% | 13% |

Changes to the company's sponsored Internet search strategy — including the use of longer-tail keywords, more targeted ad copy and campaign structures, more strategic time-of-day scheduling, and the implementation of daily cost ceilings — helped reduce the cost per lead from $56 per lead observed in the first six months of 2006 to $44 per lead for the same period a year later.

Importantly, a higher proportion of leads were converting to sales for the Web-based version of the software package. As such, the company enjoyed a ramp-up in recurring monthly sales, which improved from six customers and 15 users at the end of August 2006 to 32 customers and 71 users at the end of June 2007.

|  | August-06 | June-07 |
|---|---|---|
| **REVENUE** | | |
| Number of Customers | 6 | 32 |
| Number of Users | 15 | 72 |
| (Less Churn) | | 1 |
| **Net Number of Users** | **15** | **71** |

[1] Yankee Group: http://www.yankeegroup.com/ResearchDocument.do?id=53519

[2] http://www.chrisbrogan.com/the-b2b-vs-b2c-thing/

[3] John Jantsch: http://www.ducttapemarketing.com/newsletters/marketingplan.html

 **Tom Kennedy** is a B2B marketing and communications executive with an MBA from Regis University in Denver. Besides his current focus on enterprise software, he has helped manage companies in the solid waste and recycling, VoIP telecom services, IT services, and financial services industries develop and implement strategies to grow awareness, sales leads and profits. A BMA Colorado member since 2005, he served as a 2010-2011 board member and was the 2009-2010 president.

# 3 | The Power of Who!
## Creating a Fully Integrated Marketing Program

Brett A. Schklar

## Who Cares?

In 15 years of marketing and sales for B2B technology companies, the main lesson this author learned is that products and services are not bought, they are sold. There is a reason that sales people in B2B are paid handsomely: It takes a lot of work to convince people within organizations to say *yes* to "the deal," especially when there are even more reasons people are likely to say *no*, or the purgatory, *not yet*.

This leads us to the role of marketing. Marketing's role surrounding the B2B sales process can be looked at in two distinct arenas: strategic and tactical. Both must be viewed in parallel, especially when looking at your marketing program in a new way.

What is this technique that allows you, the B2B marketer, to look both strategically and tactically while creating a new way to weave marketing and sales together? It's an innovative method of market mapping, planning and execution leveraging two key elements that make marketing not only the strategic leader, but the fabric of the entire organization. These two elements are the development, integration and adoption of *personas and their accompanying use cases* that align marketing, sales, customer engagement, product development and the entire company together.

## The Personas

The personas program was developed for B2B companies after this author went behind the scenes at the only remaining national big-box electronics retailer. In the break room were six posters with the faces of six very distinct personalities. Each person on the posters had a story. Each person wanted to be treated differently. Here are three examples of those personas.

Jake is a tech guru. He knows what he wants and probably knows the areas of the store. While he knows what he's looking for, he may have a hard time finding that specific thing, or may have a bit of trouble determining the right one to buy. Jake doesn't want pesky sales people bugging him. He only wants to engage with a sales person when he has a specific question or if he spends more than three minutes looking at that one shelf and grabbing a few items. When a sales associate sees an outfitted Mazda 3-series car with a customized paint job, they know it's Jake. Once he is in the store, a sales person should be nearby for Jake and only engage proactively when he is "stuck" by not being able to make a decision. Advanced tech, more power and longer usability is important to Jake.

Joan, on the other hand, is not at all tech savvy. She is intimidated by the size of the store, the large wall of flat-panel screens and would rather spend

> **Lightbulb Moment #1:**
> Why aren't B2B companies doing this every single time?

her time with her friends and artwork than at this scary place. Joan drives to the store in her Prius, which brings her great joy to drive and show off. Joan needs to be comforted and assisted as quickly as possible. She is not looking to be sold. She wants to ask the right number of questions and have someone join her on her journey to find the solution to her problem. Cost, easy problem solving and friendliness are important to Joan.

Jack is looking to solve a problem. He's not tech savvy, but knows about the technology he is using. His goal is to take as much time as he needs and ask as many questions as humanly possible to make a decision. Jack uses this process whether it's a $3 item or a $3,000 item. The pickup truck that just pulled into the parking lot clearly belongs to Jack. He wants to find that one associate who will follow him around, answer his 452 questions and not complain at all about his methodology. Personal attention, knowledge, lots of product options and patience are important to Jack.

These "people" are actually personas. They are stereotypes, profiles or even racial profiles of categories of people who walk into the front door.

Developing personas is not a new concept. B2C companies have been relying on them for years. However, B2B companies have not. In actuality, B2B companies need this more desperately than B2Cs. That led this author to the decision that every client needs this approach.

## Who's on First

This chapter is designed to make you think differently about the strategic approach of understanding your audience. The specific goal is turning these strategies into executable programs that make targeting easier, tactics more clear, and programs easier to measure and nurture.

The key strategy in this chapter is developing personas for your customers and prospects, and then taking these personas, which define the *"who"* of the marketing strategy, and developing the use cases, which tell us the *"when"* to target the marketing programs.

## Aligning Marketing and Sales

If the strategy is developed correctly, the tactics will cleanly and effectively fall into four key tactical areas, all of which fully embrace the marketing and sales relationship. These areas are designed to align and support the sales process. The following diagram shows these key areas.

**Lightbulb Moment #2:**
Why aren't we doing this for EVERY ONE of our clients?

| Sales Support Function | Awareness | Familiarity | Consideration | Purchase |
| --- | --- | --- | --- | --- |

| | Awareness | Familiarity | Consideration | Purchase |
| --- | --- | --- | --- | --- |
| | Branding and PR | Branding and PR | Branding and PR | Branding and PR |
| Client View | I have a problem and I need to research it. | I have identified my problem and how I can solve it including which vendors carry a solution. | I have created a short list of vendors for consideration. I am talking to them. | I have made a buying decision. |
| Sales Tools | • White papers<br>• Webinars that identify the problem<br>• Short educational videos | • Case Studies<br>• Webinars<br>• White papers that focus on product/solution<br>• Web pages | • Web Content<br>• Data Sheets<br>• References<br>• Sales Presentations<br>• Online Demos<br>• Sales Meetings/Calls<br>• Sales Force | • Proposals |
| Demand Generation | • White paper syndications<br>• Webinars requiring registration<br>• SEO and PPC<br>• Speaking Engagements | • SEO and PPC<br>• Events like trade shows, seminars and road shows<br>• Registration programs for marketing materials<br>• E-mail Marketing | • SEO and PPC<br>• Product Videos<br>• Reference Videos | |

In order to support the sales team in the full spectrum of marketing tactics, find the gaps in these key areas.

**Awareness:** Are you a household name to your target audience? Are the people who need to know about you aware of you?

**Familiarity:** Are the targeted audiences not only aware of the capability you have, but also what makes you different, better or a better ROI?

**Consideration:** What tools are in place to help target audiences compare your solution against the competition? Do you know how to compete not just against competitors, but also competing forces such as indecision or doing it themselves?

**Purchase:** What tools help make the purchasing process faster, easier and more likely to result in a sale?

Now think about the marketing tactics that support the selling process.

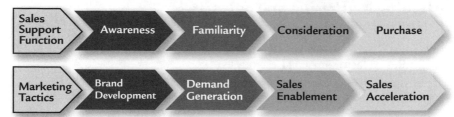

As you can see, if you are able to align the four phases of selling with the four phases of marketing, you can start to develop a common program that works in both functions and is aligned as one. Once you have this fundamental understanding, you're ready to figure out why personas and use cases are crucial to making marketing programs pack more punch.

## Who Signs a Purchase Order

Think for a moment. When one of your sales people asks for someone's signature for that big fat purchase, what goes on the signature line? Is it the company's signature or is it a company representative's signature? Who is that representative? What is their motivation? How did you get them to say yes? Who else was involved in the sale? If you know the answers to these questions, you know how to get someone to pay attention to you, your product, your service and look at you above your competition.

## Rule#1. Companies Don't Buy Stuff: People do

Seasoned, successful B2B sales people know that selling is less about the product and what it does and more about identifying the pain point of each and every contact within that organization who needs to say yes, but could potentially say no. Not only do all parties involved need to say yes, but they need to do so collectively.

> Go beyond titles and motivations. Think of a person's inherent function in his/her role: what is his/her *archetype*:
>
> **1) The President, CEO or Owner** — Decisions are made on what is best for the company. There are no politics involved or hidden agendas. Decisions are made for the good of the company.

**2) The Hired Gun** — Brought in to make decisions, implement change, start something new or get something done. Decisions are made to implement change, do something differently or implement something that has worked in the previous place of business.

**3) The Corporate Ladder Climber** — Gets the jobs done, looks good to the folks above and is burning bridges with peers and subordinates in order to make the "higher ups" happy. Decisions are made if they support his/her agenda and have him/her looked upon favorably.

**4) The Corporate Coaster** — The ultimate "9-to-5'er" who does what is needed to get the job done, no more…no less. "Change is bad" is the key mantra. Do enough to show success, but don't take on new or risky initiatives. Decisions are made based on keeping the 9-to-5 status.

## When Storytelling, Know Your Audience

*Persona: A detailed description of a fictional person that represents a group of individuals targeted by your sales and marketing effort, i.e., WHO should you care about and how should you talk about them?*

Knowing what motivates a person allows you a competitive advantage and an opportunity to accelerate the sales cycle. Take this knowledge to your marketing program. What campaign do you develop for your key client contact knowing the sales team is going into an opportunity where the participants already know your ROI story? What does the campaign say to a CFO who knows your ROI is higher than any other initiatives? What are the sales enablement tools which help the sales team demonstrate the promise of the ROI?

For the other people involved in the purchasing decision, what gets them excited enough to say yes? What makes them look good? What can marketing do to prime the pump of the solution before the sales person talks to them?

## The Use Case
### Putting the Personas into Action

*Use Case: An event or situation that causes one or more of your target personas to need your products or service, i.e. The WHERE, WHY, WHEN, HOW and WHAT of the value.*

A use case is simply when a persona will be ripe to take action. Use cases answer the following questions:

- Where did it come from?
- Why did they bring you in?
- What phase of the project cycle were they in when they talked to you?
- How did they justify the investment?
- What did they get?

## Triangulate for Accuracy

When trying to find a location of a cellular caller, you can use three cell towers to map the location through triangulation. Developing a use case strategy is similar.

Company **Direction**
Internal **Knowledge**
and **Expertise**

**Internal LENS**

**Competition**
Analysts Search &
Social Realm

The Power of
Knowing the
**Buyer's**
**Perspective**

**Triangle of Marketing Knowledge**

**Customer LENS**

**Industry LENS**

## Gaining Internal Insights

The internal knowledge of your team, while not completely objective, is invaluable in creating personas. A group of approximately four participants works best. The participants create synergy and provide more well-rounded answers. Just make sure that each participant has in-depth knowledge of your current clients.

The process includes customized exercises to meet each client situation.

1. Have the participants list their 10 largest deals, 10 most recent deals and 10 other clients (favorite, interesting, highest margins).

2. List each person at each of these companies who was part of the coalition sale.

3. List the motivators that drove each person to be receptive to the sale. List the pain points that you eliminated for each person and the goals you helped them achieve.

4. Repeat for every deal.

5. Group these deals by overlapping job titles and characteristics. There could be multiple personas for a single job title if the characteristics of professionals in that title vary significantly.

These groups represent your personas. Now, go back to the companies you listed in step one and start listing the events that caused each one of these companies to become receptive to your product or service. These events represent your use cases.

You now have preliminary personas and use cases. Use industry insights and customer information to verify and enhance the information you have generated from your internal interviews.

## Industry Intelligence

Gathering insights from industry analysts and experts who have a broader view of trends and recent events is essential and easy. With so many blogs, magazines, websites and white papers flying around, gathering insight from industry experts into your customers' pain points and goals is very easy.

## Customer Insights Through
## the Voice of the Customer (VOC)

No one can tell you more about your customers than your customers. Customer insights do two things: serve to check the insights you've gotten from other sources, and reveal new insights you've never considered. But, getting to these insights takes the right questions. Your questions need to be customized to be relevant to your clients.

## Creating a Common Company Language

If the personas and use cases are aligned with your customers and prospects — if your sales team embraces them and is incorporating this information into the fabric of the marketing and sales programs — then something interesting will happen: all people who connect with your prospects and customers will start using the same language. Product development will use these personas to map features to potential users and use cases. Customer support will map their responses to the type of person calling in. Even the CEO might segment the addressable marketplace based on the personas. Creating the company's common language around the personas creates a harmony that allows organizations to work together.

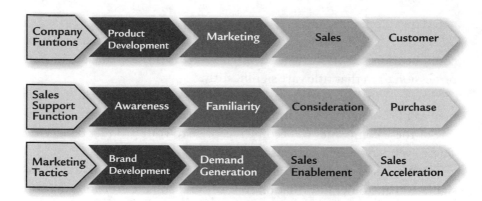

## How to Turn This Into a Marketing Program

- Start simple. Try implementing the personas as drop-downs within your CRM (customer relationship management) system or as targeted campaigns/landing pages within your MAS (marketing automation system).
- Create a messaging platform that is based on each of these personas. Develop a story for each of the use cases.
- Create a competitive landscape that addresses how competitors will try to reach each persona and use case scenario.
- Recommend a set of tactics after persona and use case development. Recommend at least 50 tactics that can be easily executed.

When developing a program, incorporate the four elements that ensure the market map is executed with a comprehensive approach: Strategy, Planning, Execution, Next.

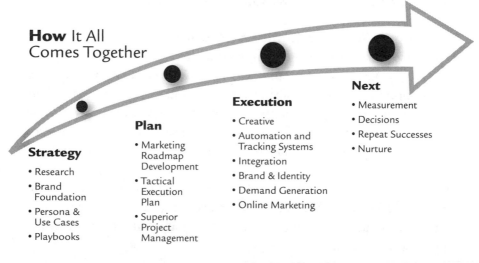

## Shifting Ain't That Easy

There will be times when the use case and persona processes are adopted religiously and other times when the company rejects these concepts. Thinking of your customer base as groups of individuals vs. companies and company segmentation is not easy to swallow. As a marketer, you need to know how to sell this to the organization. This is just as important as the personas and use cases themselves.

## CASE STUDY
## Global Software Company

**The Challenge.** A large global software company was struggling with growth in the mining industry and looking to branch out into other industries. The mining industry is fairly incestuous, where most company executives know competing company executives. This company had done an excellent job in growing within mining, but realized that in order to continue growing, it had to penetrate new markets.

**The Client.** A large global software company focused on optimization within the mining, energy, transportation and utilities industries.

**The Journey.** The company hired a new vice president of marketing who wanted to develop a new way of implementing marketing programs. This VP wanted a way to directly connect with sales activities and ensure an engaging method of creating a market map.

**The Discovery.** The Market Creation Group (MCG) was hired by the company after a colleague saw a presentation on personas and use cases.

**The Solution.** The company asked MCG to develop a comprehensive market map to rethink how to develop marketing strategies, programs and sales support to penetrate these new markets.

The first step was to understand the customer's real pain point, if it was addressable, and what resources were

*"The first step was to understand the customer's real pain point..."*

available or needed in order to achieve the aggressive goals. Once that was determined, MCG followed its long-standing tradition of making the client pitch them first to determine if the company could work with MCG and truly needed the significant amount of support requested.

**The Implementation.** Before considering personas and use cases, MCG conducted a full-day strategy lab with the client's key executives to uncover the company's direction, key differentiators, key messaging tenants, go-to-marketing plan and competitive environment. Once this was completed, MCG went on a research expedition to find all industry analyst information, competitors' research, and blogosphere and discussion group posts to gain a solid understanding of the industry. Next, MCG conducted both qualitative and quantitative research within the customer base to validate the "ivory tower" beliefs.

After completing the preliminaries, MCG developed the market map. This map incorporated key elements of the plan: personas, use cases, go-to market planning, messaging and positioning. Demand generation/sales acceleration tactics were developed along with a cohesive plan to implement these strategies and tactics into the CRM and marketing automation systems. MCG was also asked to provide ongoing services by developing a new Web presence, managing the marketing automation system, providing content development services, developing sales acceleration tools, and providing ongoing measurement and recommendations to their marketing program.

**The Results.** Without a significant increase in marketing spend, the client was able to fully roll out this program, provide highly targeted marketing programs and have tighter alignment with the sales organization. Response rates went from averages of 10 percent to new averages of 22 percent. And, the average sales cycle was reduced by 18 percent.

**Brett Schklar** is founder and chief marketing officer of The Market Creation Group (MCG), the nation's premiere B2B technology-focused marketing firm that provides in-depth marketing strategy, project management and demand generation. He is a recognized entrepreneur and was the recipient of the Denver Business Journal's Forty Under 40 award in 2010. He is an adjunct professor at the University of Denver, Daniels College of Business, teaching various marketing courses. Brett has been a BMA Colorado member since 2007.

# 4 | Expand Your Pipeline Through Integrated Teleprospecting

Orlin Camerlo

This chapter outlines best practices currently being utilized to drive strong pipeline opportunities through targeted integrated teleprospecting campaigns. It focuses on why and how to improve your campaign results by integrating telemarketing. The chapter focuses on integrated marketing tactics for new client acquisition as opposed to marketing to customers. However, most of these tactics will also work for existing customers with slight modifications.

## Why Integrate Your Teleprospecting With E-Mail and/or Direct Mail Marketing Efforts

Today's typical decision maker is exposed to more communication methods, technologies and tactics than at any other time in history. It's common to receive 100 to 200 e-mails a day on top of instant messages, phone calls and mobile texts. Most executives and corporate decision makers are currently responsible for multiple positions within their organization and rarely have blocks of time to explore or be educated on new services, technologies, products or solutions that may make their companies more successful.

Marketers continue to struggle with how to cut through the world of over-communication. Integrated marketing opens up an interesting long-term marketing tactic that can yield significant results. Using multiple touches to communicate to executives can improve marketing effectiveness. Many executives still open their own mail and respond well to messages that reflect cost savings or growth for their organizations.

Not surprisingly, contacting prospects by phone immediately after their exposure to the direct marketing touch can open up an interesting conversation and present new pipeline opportunities. One long-term benefit is that marketers have a cleaned database that is even more targeted for future touches. Timing is crucial, so consistently utilizing integrated marketing tactics with teleprospecting can keep your value proposition in front of key decision makers. Also, targeting a prospect with consistent messages and multiple touches allows for more success when it comes to defined outcomes, such as meeting face-to-face with the prospect.

> *"Timing is crucial, so consistently utilizing integrated marketing tactics with teleprospecting can keep your value proposition in front of key decision makers."*

## How to Integrate Traditional Marketing With Teleprospecting

Your database is critical. Too many companies fail to thoroughly evaluate their internal databases and prioritize their top new business accounts from the rest. Many companies take a lackadaisical approach, compiling a database from their sales team of random former customers or contacts and ending up marketing repeatedly to the same prospect list without getting results. This can be an expensive proposition.

Companies also fail to confirm whether contacts are still viable within their targeted new business accounts. They fail to confirm where decisions are made — a remote satellite office or a headquarters location. It's worthwhile spending the time to refine the list within the budget and campaign timeframes. Direct mail and e-mail can be very helpful with this process.

### Database 101: Best Practices for Teleprospecting

Marketers have many tactical data options at their disposal. However, spending time on this crucial aspect of an integrated teleprospecting project is often overlooked. If you are in a position to score, segment or further evaluate your data there are some really simple steps that can be taken to dramatically improve your goals and outcomes. Ask questions before beginning any teleprospecting efforts:

- What level are you targeting?
- Do you have two segmented groups to target (Tier I prospects vs. Tier II prospects)?
- Does your direct mail work with the teleprospecting messaging?
- Are you keeping it simple? Can people quickly conclude what you want them to do?

- Who will take the appointments and what is the process?
- What type of accounts are you marketing to according to your plan: new target accounts, warm prospects, former customers, active customers?

## Building a Constructive and Useful Value Proposition

Do you remember the last time you received an incoherent or poorly targeted cold call or direct mail piece that confused or alienated you? Oftentimes we want to include everything but the kitchen sink in our messaging because we have so many exciting features, functions and value to share. Instead, define a constructive, simple and value-oriented message using these best practices:

- Create value propositions that hit quickly and effectively around saving or making the prospect money.
- Build messaging that engages the prospect in dialogue and creates instant clarity on why you are marketing to them.
- Utilize one defined and consistent value proposition for all integration tactics (such as e-mail, direct mail, etc.) to be more productive and successful.

## Marketplace Evaluation and Feedback

No one likes to be criticized or constantly evaluated. However, as marketers we have to keep ourselves honest on integration tactics to determine if they are truly working. We have to be our own worst critics. Several questions need to be asked early on in your campaign to help you stay honest with the projected outcomes:

- How are you tracking long-term opportunities as compared to short-term appointments that may lead to opportunities?
- What is the marketplace relaying? Are there specific competitors you are running into?
- Are you focused on the right decision makers?
  - Are there trends on who is taking to your message?
    Are there trends or data points on why they are not interested?
  - How can you evaluate the quality of the feedback you are receiving from the teleprospecting effort?

## Iterative Process Best Practice

You should always continue to evaluate your process even after you receive initial results or successes:

- What are the results of the first few meetings?
  - What can you change to alter outcomes?

· What is the call to action?
- What are the outcomes of the folks who were not interested? Is there valuable information within this data for future integrated marketing campaigns?

## Overall Results and Key Metrics

We often assume that the simple metric goals are good enough to consider the campaign a success. However, a true best practice is to evaluate further and to consider follow-on tactics. Utilize the following questions:
- Close the loop with sales — what has entered the pipeline? What leads need to be nurtured?
- Are there trends you can capture in that territory, marketplace or industry?
- What nurturing tactics are needed (e-mail and direct mail or the occasional check-in call) now that they are confirmed?

## CASE STUDY
## Integrated Campaign Results

**The Challenge.** ABC Company wanted to know how to increase qualified opportunities for the sales team and quickly develop new business.

**The Client.** An award-winning, national open systems integrator with several decades of experience partnered with Extended Presence, a teleprospecting firm, to generate interest and set appointments with targeted prospects. As a national open systems integrator, ABC Company provides comprehensive consulting services, successful storage and data management solutions, assessments, and implementation services to help customers meet today's IT and business challenges. In particular, ABC focuses on customizing unique solutions and successfully addressing companies' particular IT challenges. As a consistent member of the VAR Business Top 500, ABC pursues active involvement in the industry, maintaining the highest level of engineering certifications with partners and the vendor community.

**The Journey.** Multiple, non-integrated marketing efforts from different vendors had been implemented with nominal success before the hiring of Extended Presence. Direct mail was delivering results as were teleprospecting efforts. However, the sales team was not engaged in deciding what accounts to specifically target. Inconsistent data being utilized were a random collection of prospects. No long-term strategy was in place and prospects were not getting touched multiple times because campaigns were in separate silos.

**The Discovery.** ABC had not worked with an integrated organization that utilized multiple tactics and integration in campaign execution. ABC needed this type solution due to the sophisticated nature of their services and solutions.

**The Solution.** The integrated campaign was developed and promoted with buy-in from the sales team who provided the lists. The information was scrubbed, new contacts were added and obsolete contacts (nearly one-third of their list) were removed. In comparison to a single-touch appointment-setting effort, this campaign consisted of dimensional and unique direct mail packaging, timely HTML touches and follow-up calling.

**The Results.** Through this integrated teleprospecting effort, 37 percent more appointments were set for the sales team. Just under a 40 percent increase in projected sales pipeline was developed. This led to over $35 million in pipeline being developed that quarter. The keys to success in this effort were:
- Refined and nurtured integrated data
- Close integration around the direct mail results
- Strategic teleprospecting best practices

According to the client's marketing director, "The campaign not only helped get our sales people appointments with the right prospects, but also reinforced our branding in the marketplace. Thanks to integration, these prospects will think of us first when they're ready to commit."

## Conclusion

There are three main elements that make integrated teleprospecting work. Make sure you put them to work for you.

**1. Prospect list.** Fifty percent or more of a campaign's success is directly tied to the prospect list. To ensure that your data are as up-to-date as possible, conduct a cleansing effort on the delivered list. In addition, ask your sales team to provide fresh prospects.

**2. Messages.** Your targeted prospects are bombarded by marketing messages every day so it is paramount that your communications get noticed. Create themed pre- and-post digital communications and "can't miss" direct mail that provide prospects with multiple ways to respond, with enticing incentives and with messaging that hits upon their pain points.

**3. Follow-up.** Timing is crucial for telemarketing. Scheduling prompt follow-up while awareness and interest are at its peak is critical. The integrated approach greatly decreases the appointment-setting cycle — which means that your sales team gets in front of their target prospects faster.

**Orlin Camerlo** is the current CEO of Extended Presence. Since 2007, he has increased EP's revenues by 250 percent. Under his leadership, EP has developed over 600 individual marketing campaigns that drive over $500 million in pipeline value. Prior to EP, Orlin was involved with diverse technology and telecom organizations. He is a very active volunteer with the mentoring organization, Denver Kids Inc. Orlin is a graduate of the University of Northern Colorado. He has been a member of BMA Colorado since 2007.

# 5 | Keys to Creating a Successful Customer-Retention Plan

Lisa A. Miller

A s marketers, we are constantly challenged by how we spend our time and resources. One debate we consistently are challenged by is do we spend more on customer retention or customer acquisition? In other words, should more of your marketing budget be spent finding new customers or should it be spent keeping the ones you have? Should you allocate more of your time and resources to one vs. the other? In reality, you can't do one without the other.

While customer acquisition can be more time consuming, energy draining and expensive than classic customer retention activities — some studies suggest it costs between five and seven times as much as

> **"Today's economic climate necessitates extra efforts to keep the best of the best clients."**

maintaining a profitable relationship with an existing customer — it is still a necessary part of the business and marketing plan. Acquiring new clients is crucial due to natural churn because, for whatever reason, your current customers will leave your business. Whether it is because a new competitor has arrived on the scene, the customer has left the business or they are no longer satisfied with your product, even the best customers leave eventually. You have no choice but to replace those valuable customers if you want to continue to grow your business.

On the other hand, a customer-retention plan, called by various names such as a client-loyalty plan or a client-communications plan, is a crucial component to any marketing plan and one that can easily be overlooked for its perceived complexity. This chapter is designed to make the task simpler and more enriching to the overall sales cycle. Today's economic climate necessitates extra efforts to keep the best of the best clients.

## Four Steps to Developing a Customer-Retention Plan

Customer-retention activities are different in different markets. For example, in the retail environment (restaurant, book store, beauty salon, etc.) they could include a "buy 12 and get the next free" card for their customers. For a grocery store, it could mean a "club" card that offers additional discounts and special offers. But what if you are in charge of marketing a purely service-oriented business in a highly regulated industry? I'm going to review a few of the best practices I have used successfully while consulting in the financial services industry. Although the examples and situations are from the financial services industry, they can be easily translated to many different markets.

## Step 1. Who do You Want to Retain?

What did you do yesterday to prepare your business for a successful tomorrow? How often do you engage with your most profitable clients? Do you have processes in place to automatically communicate to your clients?

To begin, every marketer knows there is only so much money in the checkbook and so much time in a day. A great marketer takes that knowledge and creates a purposeful, systematic approach to his customer-retention programs. The first step is to determine which clients, or types of clients, should be retained. It may sound like a very basic concept, but it is one frequently overlooked.

In deciding which customers to retain and to replicate, let's start with the 80/20 rule. According to Wikipedia, the 80/20 rule is a principle that was suggested by management-thinker Joseph M. Juran. It was named after the Italian economist Vilfredo Pareto who observed that 80 percent of income in Italy was received by 20 percent of the Italian population. The assumption is that most of the results in any situation are determined by a small number of causes.

If you haven't done so recently, review your client list to determine which 20 percent of your customers are the most valuable and bring in 80 percent of the revenue. Does the 80/20 rule apply? Your task is to segment your client base and find out.

### Case Study Example

For purposes of clarification, this case study uses a financial advisor, but these principles would be appropriate for any service oriented provider/sales representative. Our financial advisor, Ben, has had a successful practice for eight years. Although he could describe his career as successful, he knows that if nothing changes and he doesn't grow his business he will soon be closing his doors. At the very least, he will hit a plateau and no longer have the energy or the passion to continue. So Ben is on a mission this year: to strengthen the relationships he has with his top 20 percent of clients and then, to find more like them.

Ben begins by defining his ideal client. What would he do? What would he be interested in? What would his needs be? What are Ben's business goals for the year? What industry-specific situations can bring Ben the most value? The combined answers to these questions create his "ideal client."

Ultimately Ben's ideal client — the client that he would enjoy working with and to whom he can add significant value — would be those individuals who are local business owners, are active in their communities, have children or grandchildren and see Ben as a well-respected member of their advisory team. These criteria define his ideal A+ client or A+ prospect (which is the first client model we will reference).

Once the ideal client was defined, we outlined the attributes of other client models as well starting with his A+ client (the ideal client definition). Then Ben detailed the definitions for the other client models: the A client, B, and finally, the C client.

### After Creating the Definition, the Search Begins

The next step is to review the entire client list and begin identifying the clients by the various rankings.

As a side note, some marketers would argue that the best and fastest way to do this is to review a list of the top 20 clients by profitability and disregard the questions posed earlier. While it is the fastest way to segment for your best clients, it is not the best way. What if, of the top 20 clients, 15 are already spending as much as they ever will with you? What if one or two don't treat you or your team members appropriately? What if you dread their calls? While you certainly don't want to lose them, do you really want to invest additional resources with them?

### Step 2. Segment Your Clients

With your ideal prospect definition nearby, begin by using a clean list of all your clients (hard-copy or electronic) with information that is pertinent to your business and that will enable you to identify to which model each client belongs. For example, with Ben, our client list spreadsheet included name, address, name of business, if they were an owner, and children's names and ages. In other words, he included the database information that would identify the clients that had the greatest potential to help him reach his goals next year.

Ben segmented his clients/book of business with a fresh set of eyes and focused on the above information while including intrinsic characteristics such as their loyalty, value, experience, and influence. Ben reviewed his list by asking the following questions:

- Loyalty: how long have they been an active customer?
- Value (value vs. profitability): What is their value in the long-term? Will they refer others to you? Do they have future potential? Is their business growing or have they plateaued or worse?
- Experience: What has been your experience with them? Has it been extremely positive? Or just moderately positive? Has their business experienced some of the same challenges/issues you have, and have they come out of that with a new knowledge base? Can you learn from them and their experiences?
- Influence: What influence do they have within your industry or within your future client's industry? What influence do they have in your community?

**An Art, not a Science**

This exercise would be easier if it were a science. But few marketing activities are — they are an art. This activity is certainly an art and intuition needs to be considered.

As Ben reviewed his client list, client by client, he identified whether they were an A+/A, B or C client — based on the criteria he set.

After indicating which "bucket" they belong in, Ben created a separate list of just his A+ and A clients (the rest of the clients would also go through this process, but we began with his A+/A clients). These are the individuals who have the greatest potential for helping him grow his business and this is where he will spend the majority of his time and resources.

**Step 3. Identify How You Can Add the Most Value to These Clients**

The next step is to identify what you can do to add the most value to these "platinum" clients. Start by asking the following questions:

- What is their preferred method for communication (i.e., social networks, e-mail, phone, text, snail mail)?
- What information do they want to learn more about?

• What are their interests? Passions? Goals?

• How can you help?

Sales representatives sometimes choose to uncover this type of information via an e-mail survey. At our recommendation, Ben chose to uncover the answers to these questions in person. He scheduled a breakfast or lunch meeting with each of his A+ clients for the purpose of getting to know these valued clients better. He came prepared with a list of questions in his mind that he wove into a conversation: What do they like to read (i.e., magazines, blogs, professional journals, books, etc.)? What are their hobbies? What non-profits or civic activities are they involved in? What boards do they serve on? Do they like to travel? Where is their next vacation destination? What is their favorite restaurant? What are their personal and/or professional goals for the next three years?

## Step 4. Create a Client-Loyalty Plan Based on the Answers

During these enjoyable conversations, Ben uncoverd the following:

1. Of his 27 A+/Platinum clients, 15 of them love to read action-packed thrillers. When a well-known author came to town, he invited his clients (and a guest) to attend the lecture with him and his wife. He also arranged a pre-lecture gathering across the street for light appetizers and cocktails.

2. One of his A+ clients is a wine connoisseur — and has an appreciation for a very specific vineyard in Italy. For this client's 10-year anniversary of opening his successful business, Ben went to the local wine store and found a bottle from the vineyard. Upon receiving the bottle, the client was not only impressed by the gesture but also that Ben had listened and retained interest in his passions.

3. One of his clients is very involved with a local non-profit that hosts a gala event annually. This year, Ben bought a corporate table and invited other clients to attend with him. All were impressed.

4. Several of his clients attend a weekly outdoor jazz concert in their neighborhood. For the final concert of the season, Ben set a nice table with linens, flowers, snacks, cheese & crackers, wine, beer, soda, etc. and invited his clients to stop by before, during or after the event. They appreciated having a central meeting place where they could come and go as they pleased.

5. His clients want more information about what is happening with the economy. Ben made sure all of his clients were included as subscribers to his monthly newsletter.

## Summary

Ben asked questions and then listened. By doing this he uncovered more about his clients than he ever knew. His customer-retention plan was wildly successful. These clients were impressed by Ben's thoughtfulness and responded with more referrals and more business than they ever had before.

There are plenty of ideas to consider for your customer-retention plan. Here are a few to get you started:

1. A hand-written note in a birthday or thank you card goes a long way.

2. Find an unexpected holiday to celebrate with your best clients. For example, if you know your clients love the arts, celebrate Picasso's birthday by taking a few clients to join you on a guided tour at your local art museum to view his work. Or buy a coffee-table book of Picasso's art and send to your clients with a note.

3. Have a nice plant or flowers delivered to their business in honor of their one-year anniversary.

4. For clients with kids, order a block of tickets to the next big children's movie. Let them know that popcorn and soda are included.

The list of ideas is endless. The best place to start is always with your best clients. Additional ideas can be added, but create a plan (include a calendar) so that these great intentions don't slip through the cracks of your busy day-to-day activities.

Your clients are your competitor's prospects so make sure you give them the attention they deserve and desire. Remember, as a general rule, client retention is proportionate to client attention.

**Lisa Miller** has been the chief marketing officer at Northwestern Mutual-Denver since 2008. She has over 20 years of experience in a variety of industries including financial services, higher education, utilities and health insurance. Specifically, her background includes brand management, business development, event management, product launch, vendor relations, consultation/coaching, advertising, public relations, training, and strategic marketing plan development. A very active volunteer, she has been a member of BMA Colorado since 2009.

CHAPTER

# 6 | Successfully Managing the Customer Experience

Charles H. Patti, Ph.D.

I n the September 2010 issue of Inc. magazine, business products and services were the third largest segment among the "hottest" industries (fastest growing) in 2010, comprising 45 companies and nearly 5,500 new jobs. And, this doesn't count the B2B jobs in the other hot segments such as government services, software, IT services, financial services, telecommunications and retail. Could this impressive growth have taken place without attention to superior customer experience? Not likely. Among the lessons learned from the recent economic recession is that it's nearly impossible to survive without deep understanding of customers and delivering exceptional experiences. But, what are "experiences"? Can experiences be managed? How can we measure the return on investment (ROI) of experiences? This chapter briefly answers these questions and then provides an illustrative case history.

## The Journey of CEM

Each year, there are over 10,000 new business books published in the United States alone. That's hundreds of millions of words giving advice on a range of business topics — from leadership, to survival tactics, to marketing. Every now and then, one of these ideas rings so true that we change the way we think about and conduct business. Customer experience management (CEM) is one of those rare business ideas that is so compelling it has pushed itself through the maze of business rhetoric and risen to the forefront of business thinking. When *The Experience Economy* was published in 1999 by Joe Pine and Jim Gilmore, it became a best seller, but managers didn't immediately embrace the ideas and change their ways of doing business. Powerful ideas often take time to penetrate the way we think and how we lead our companies.

**Winning with positive emotions.** Ideas like CEM require a change in business culture, leadership, management and how we view customers. In the graduate courses taught in the Daniels College of Business at the University of Denver, we tell students that a business experience is "an economic exchange between buyer and seller in which the buyer receives a unique collection of tangible and intangible experiences that result in a positive emotional relationship with the brand and a positive feeling within the customer." Customers want to feel good when they do business with us. They want to feel proud, satisfied, cared for, confident, pampered, rewarded, appreciated, protected and any number of other powerful emotions. Sure, they want the product or service to work — but a functional product alone doesn't lead to a long-term competitive advantage. Nor does good service. Nor does a low price. These are the basic pieces of equipment to enter the game. You don't win just because you have a bat, ball and glove. You win when you capture the hearts of the customer. CEM is about learning how to touch customers deeply, making them feel so good that they want to help us find new customers and keep the ones we have. When this happens, our cost of doing business goes down because it's easier to acquire new customers, we increase the lifetime value of existing customers and we reduce customer turnover.

**From concept to maturity.** Like all new business concepts, CEM continues to mature. From the initial ideas of Joe Pine and Jim Gilmore (*The Experience Economy*, 1999), to the writings of Bernd Schmitt (*Customer Experience Management*, 2003) and Lew Carbone (*Clued In*, 2004), CEM has moved beyond the idea stage. Constructs are emerging, frameworks for the management of CE appear in the business press, and methods for gaining greater insight into how customers feel about themselves and the brands they experience are gaining acceptance. We now accept that CEM is penetrating business leadership and practice. Companies from every sector of the economy now have CEM positions. Ideas about "maturity levels" of CEM (within companies) are being discussed. There is a lively debate about the constructs of CEM. And, CEM is being applied to all business sectors (B2C, B2B, not-for-profit, etc.) and across all stakeholder groups (see *Firms of Endearment*, Sisodia et al, 2007).

## What are Experiences?
**Four dimensions build an emotional connection.** Beyond the stated definition, CEM consists of four dimensions that are critical to creat-

ing positive experiences for customers. The four dimensions are shown in Figure 1. Note that the dimensions all contribute to the emotional connection that is created with customers — and, the dimensions are related to each other. For example, "what we say" overlaps considerably with "people & culture" and with "our look & feel."

**Figure 1: The Four Dimensions of Customer Experience Management**

## Examples of the Four CEM Dimensions

At this point in the development of CEM, four dimensions have emerged as essential in creating an emotional reaction from customers.

## Functionality (What We Do)

Long considered the single most important reason that buyers work with specific B2B sellers, functionality has to do with the core product/service provided. In the B2B sector, this includes the performance quality of products/services; strength of distribution system; R&D capability; delivery and installation capabilities; engineering and design strength; skill level of customer service representatives; etc.

## Ambiance (Our Look and Feel)

Although we most often associate the relevance of look and feel with consumer goods and services (e.g., restaurants, hotels, department stores, online businesses, airlines), it is also important in the B2B sector where it includes appearance of company representatives; the appearance and convenience of office space; product packaging (where applicable); etc.

## Communication (What We Say)

In recent years, communication has taken on increased importance in the B2B sector and it now includes all forms of mass, selective and interpersonal media, including advertising in traditional media, e.g., broadcast, print, direct mail; website, social media, mobile media; call centers and face-to-face messages through company representatives. The communication dimension includes media used; the nature of messages, including sincerity and accuracy; timeliness; and tone.

## Leadership (Our People and Culture)

The rise of communication technology has fueled even more interest in the effect of people and culture on the customer experience. Most of the companies in MSN Money's Customer Service Hall of Shame are woefully short on people and culture. The biggest shortcomings include not answering phone calls, not delivering on promises, not listening to customers, not dealing with complaints, not being helpful and proactive, and not training staff to be knowledgeable problem solvers. It's no secret that customers feel good about themselves when the brand delivers on these basic people and culture components. Yet, negative customer experiences are most often attributed to staff shortcomings.

## Can Experiences Be Managed?

**Closing the experience gap.** Although experiences reside in the mind and heart of the customer, marketers can create the opportunity for the best possible experience outcome. This is accomplished by continuous efforts to close the "experience gap" — the gap between the desired experience of the customer and the experience delivered by the seller (Figure 2). To do this, sellers need to have a deep understanding of customers: how they feel about the product category, your brand, and themselves. This is accomplished through a variety of research methods, including those that tap into the affective (emotional) dimensions of customer behavior. For example, in recent years, the Zaltman Metaphor Elicitation Technique (ZMET) has been gaining ground in providing this type of understanding to sellers.

*"...marketers can create the opportunity for the best possible experience outcome."*

Figure 2: The Experience Gap

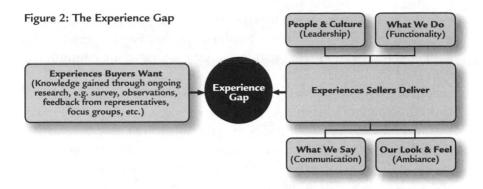

**Leading a company to higher profits through CEM.** Engaging in research to understand the desired experience of customers is one of two foundations to successfully managing customer experiences. The other foundation is embracing the experience path to long-term profits. As shown in Figure 3, this path is grounded in the idea that a deep emotional connection with customers is the key marketplace differentiator (again, recall CEM's rejection of the "better product, lower price" and the "efficiency/cost reduction" models of business). This differentiator will result in higher levels of customer loyalty and advocacy. Such loyalty and advocacy reduces the cost of acquiring new customers, extends the lifetime value of customers and reduces customer turnover. Of course, every business should strive to minimize inefficiency, but in the end, profits are created by understanding customers and meeting their needs better than competitors.

Figure 3: The CEM Road to Higher Profits

## Relevance of CEM to the B2B Marketplace: What is the ROI of CEM?

Over the past 50+ years, there has been no shortage of marketing ideas — the "4Ps," "the marketing concept," "Positioning," "One-to-One Marketing," "CRM," and "IMC" are just a few of the most widely known and discussed. Most marketing ideas fade into marketing history books eventually. The main reason for this lack of wide scale, enduring adoption is the lack of proof of contribution to profits. For example, can we demonstrate that an investment in integrated marketing communication (IMC) will generate profits beyond the cost? Marketers in all sectors have been notably unsuccessful in demonstrating marketing ROI (MROI). Only in the realm of direct marketing, including online marketing, have ideas of cost-benefits been demonstrated. But, even within these directly observable, measurable environments there is controversy about the long-term effects of this measurable, transaction-oriented approach on brand building. The test of the staying power of CEM depends on the ability to measure its ROI.

## CASE STUDY
## Tiger Communications: The challenge of the CEM investment

**The Client.** Tiger Communications is a broadband telecommunications company operating in South Carolina, North Carolina, and Virginia. The company delivers high-speed Internet, video-on-demand, HD television, and digital telephone to residential and business customers. Its B2B services include voice and Internet products and services. Tiger has about 120,000 residential subscribers and about 25,000 business customers. Tiger was founded in 1990 and during its relatively short history gained a solid reputation for high-quality service. In fact, the company won several awards for its service.

**The Challenge.** Tiger is independently owned, profitable and enjoys an excellent reputation in the community, with its employees, suppliers, and residential and business customers. During the past five years, the company has been struggling to compete with larger, national companies that have been entering its marketplace. These competitors have focused on attracting Tiger's business customers through aggressive marketing — primarily price cutting and extensive advertising. The most alarming result of the competitive activity is the declining percentage of Tiger business customers who are voice and Internet customers (Table 1). This segment — internally known as the "Dynamic Duo" segment — is nearly three times more profitable than the voice-only or Internet-only segments. Also, the Dynamic Duo segment has a much higher retention rate than the voice-only or Internet-only segments.

**Table 1: Composition of Tiger Business Customers (2005-2009)**

| YEAR | VOICE & INTERNET CUSTOMERS | % of TOTAL BUSINESS CUSTOMERS | VOICE- OR INTERNET- ONLY CUSTOMERS | % of TOTAL BUSINESS CUSTOMERS | TOTAL BUSINESS CUSTOMERS |
|------|------|------|------|------|------|
| 2009 | 11,192 | 45% | 13,680 | 55% | 24,872 |
| 2008 | 12,307 | 48% | 13,333 | 52% | 25,640 |
| 2007 | 13,485 | 51% | 12,957 | 49% | 26,442 |
| 2006 | 16,107 | 58% | 11,664 | 42% | 27,771 |
| 2005 | 17,920 | 62% | 10,982 | 38% | 28,902 |

**The Journey.** Twice each year, Tiger measures its customer experience through the Net Promoter Score (NPS). The company believes there is a relationship between NPS and sales and profits. Given the increased competition in the business segment and the declining number of Dynamic Duo customers, Tiger considered a sizeable investment in the experience they deliver to business customers. After exploring several alternatives, Tiger invested in a training program to enhance the skills of its business sales representatives. The training focused on better hiring practices, increased range of skills of the sales representatives and better career opportunities for the representatives. The overall idea was that better sales representatives would help increase the NPS and, in turn, sales and profits would increase. The cost to implement the new training and motivation program was $250,000.

**The Results.** At six and twelve months after the new customer-experience program was in place, Tiger looked at the results (Table 2). While the company was pleased, it wondered if the investment was justified. Should it invest another $250,000? How could Tiger evaluate the impact of the enhanced customer experience? How much would it have to invest to get back to the "good old days" of 2005?

**Table 2: Results of Tiger Investment in Customer Experience**

| YEAR | VOICE & INTERNET CUSTOMERS | % of TOTAL BUSINESS CUSTOMERS | VOICE- OR INTERNET- ONLY CUSTOMERS | % of TOTAL BUSINESS CUSTOMERS | TOTAL BUSINESS CUSTOMERS |
|------|------|------|------|------|------|
| July-Dec (2009) | 12,048 | 48% | 13,304 | 52% | 25,102 |
| Jan-June 2010 | 11,402 | 47% | 12,858 | 53% | 24,260 |

## CEM and B2B Marketing: Next Steps

**The Situation.** The Tiger Communications case does not completely answer the ultimate question for management: Was the $250,000 investment justified? Among the unknown issues are: what is the exact profitability of the Dynamic Duo segment; how much did the NPS improve; what is the lifetime value of individual customers in both sectors; and, what other customer experience improvement might have been more profitable? Tiger's new training program embraced only one of the four CEM dimensions (Functionality and possibly Leadership). Perhaps they would have had a greater return if they had invested in Communication or Look and Feel. The point is that a deep analysis is required to make definitive judgments about CEM investments.

A full-scale commitment to CEM is not easy and often requires an organizational culture shift. While corporate cultures are often difficult to change, much is gained by thinking about a CEM maturity journey (Table 3) in which the journey begins with Knowledge about CEM, its dimensions and measurement issues. Following that is a Commitment to CEM, which involves communicating the value of CEM throughout the organization and implementing selective aspects of CEM practice. Finally, full-scale Implementation is achieved when every member of the organization embraces CEM and is totally committed to building emotional bonds with customers.

**Table 3: CEM Maturity Curve**

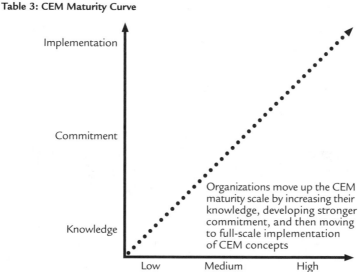

Organizations move up the CEM maturity scale by increasing their knowledge, developing stronger commitment, and then moving to full-scale implementation of CEM concepts

Advocates of CEM realize there are levels of customer experience. Hotels, airlines, car rental companies and financial services are just a few B2C industries that offer different levels of customer experience, e.g., bronze, silver, and gold levels. The same leveling of CEM takes place in the B2B sector. More profitable customers (the Dynamic Duo segment within Tiger Communications, for instance) will receive a higher level of customer experience than the voice- or data-only customers. The key is to understand the experience that makes your customers feel good when they engage with you.

Carbone, Lewis P. *Clued In: How to Keep Customers Coming Back Again and Again*. Upper Saddle River, New Jersey: Pearson Education, 2004.

"How They Stack Up," *Inc.*, September 2010, p. 111.

Olson, Jerry. "Understanding Customer Experience," *Customer Experience Management: Lessons and Insights for the Cable Industry*, edited by Jana Henthorn, Charles H. Patti, and Ronald Rizzuto. Rockville, Maryland: CableFax/Access Intelligence, 2010.

Pine, II, B. Joseph, and James H. Gilmore. *The Experience Economy: Work is Theatre & Every Business a Stage*. Boston, Massachusetts: Harvard Business School Press, 1999.

Reicheld, Frederick. "The One Number You Need to Grow," *Harvard Business Review*. December 2003.

Schmitt, Bernd. *Customer Experience Management: A revolutionary approach to connecting with your customer*. New York: John Wiley & Sons, Inc., 2003.

Sisodia, Rajendra S., David B. Wolfe, and Jagdish N. Sheth. *Firms of Endearment: How World-Class Companies Profit from Passion and Purpose*. Upper Saddle River, New Jersey: Wharton School Publishing, 2007.

Zaltman, Gerald. *How Customers Think: Essential Insights Into the Mind of the Market*. Boston, Massachusetts: Harvard Business School Press, 2003.

**Charles H. Patti** is the James M. Cox Professor of Customer Experience Management at the Daniels College of Business, University of Denver. He has a long career in B2B marketing and higher education — as a faculty member, senior executive, consultant, and author of dozens of articles and cases, books and industry reports. Professor Patti has extensive international experience, including visiting professorships in Finland, Italy, England, New Zealand, Singapore, and Malaysia. Prior to rejoining the University of Denver in 2006, he was the Head of the School of Advertising, Marketing, and Public Relations at Queensland University of Technology, Brisbane, Australia. In addition to this academic position, Dr. Patti has an active profile in industry through consulting, boards, collaborations, and expert witness assignments. Dr. Patti was a long-time BMA Colorado member in the 1980s and rejoined in 2008.

# 7 | Five Critical Success Factors for Entrepreneurs

Larry Brummond

T here are five intangible factors that can greatly influence the success of a business. This chapter is a summary of the five factors and how they impact a B2B company. Although the ideas presented here are primarily directed at entrepreneurs, any business manager can benefit as well. A B2B case study is included to help business owners and executives capture and integrate the five factors in their businesses.

## Success is More Than Just Numbers

Business owners or aspiring entrepreneurs must have a solid understanding of the numbers — sales projections, capital requirements, expenses, and profit goals. However, there are five factors having little to do with the numbers that could have just as great an impact on the success (or failure) of that business.

1. Know your entrepreneurial personality.
2. Fully understand the level of responsibility involved.
3. Understand and set goals.
4. Establish steadfast values inside your business.
5. Get and keep the right attitude.

In good or "normal" economic times it takes more than knowledge of a product or service and accounting help to be a successful entrepreneur. In tough times it's doubly important to call on all the resources available. In the B2B world, these factors should be embraced and applied by owners and executives. It sets the tone for strong, trusting business relationships, something particularly crucial for entrepreneurial companies.

## Success Factor 1. Know Your Entrepreneurial Personality

Through personal experience, it became clear that entrepreneurial personalities should be compatible with ownership structure: sole proprietor, family, or non-family partnerships. A sole proprietor I've dubbed "The Lone Stranger." Someone who wants family involvement is "The Family Gatherer." An entrepreneur who seeks non-family partners to share both financial and functional burdens is called "The Painless Partner." For this chapter, partner and partnership are used in a generic, co-owner sense, not as a legal structure term.

Each of these organizational structures requires personality types with strengths that match the dynamics of that structure: not just technical skills, but leadership, management, and organizational skills. It's about understanding the intangibles. Most importantly, it's about decision making and understanding your own ego.

*"It's about understanding the intangibles. Most importantly, it's about decision making and understanding your own ego."*

"The Lone Stranger" needs diverse management and organizational skills. He must be able to cope with higher levels of responsibility, be a better time manager and a whiz at multi-tasking.

"The Painless Partner" or "Family Gatherer" has others to share the load, but having multiple owners means additional interaction challenges. Any partnership, family or otherwise, requires individuals capable of putting egos aside in crucial decision-making situations. Those with overactive egos will not make good partners.

*"Each of these organizational structures requires personality types with strengths that match the dynamics of that structure."*

The family partnership has more implications because of the personal relationships. Non-family partnerships get into trouble because partners fail to establish hard and fast rules about decision making. With family partnerships, business issues can easily spill over into personal disputes. Making sure disagreements can be resolved swiftly and amicably, while keeping egos in check, is the biggest challenge for all partnerships. Here's a decision-making table you can use as a guide.

## A Business Guide to Decision Making

Decision making is a key component to being an effective manager and a good leader. There are plenty of good, common sense approaches and processes to decision making. One process, for example, might include defining the problem, gathering the facts, reviewing options and outcomes, brainstorming and proper follow up. Anyone in a decision-making role can develop a reasonable process that fits their situation and is appropriate for the nature of their business.

Here are three simple rules that can work whether you're running a division, department or an entire company.

| Rule | Issues | Solutions |
|---|---|---|
| Clearly define the hierarchy of decision making. | Misinterpreted or mismanaged decision process; uncertainty as to who makes the final decision. | Don't just assume everyone knows. Major decisions (strategic or policy) are the domain of managers, executives and/or owners. Delegate day-to-day operational decisions as much as possible to supervisors, project leads or even line staff. |
| Establish a discussion forum for major (policy, strategic) decisions. | Who will be involved. | Limit a forum to those who must carry out (implement) the decision. Those indirectly affected can be informed of decisions, but need not participate in the forum. |
| | Time elements. | Control how much time will be spent on the discussion and when a final decision will be made. |
| | The process. | Decide who presides over the forum. The steps might be: open discussion, presentations, documentation, outcome review. |
| | The final decision. | May be obvious once the discussion and presentation process has been completed. Decision is confirmed with informal vote or made by the person who has been assigned primary responsibility. |
| Establish a decision support culture – a philosophy – a mindset. | Not unanimous agreement. | Get every team member's support, whether in agreement or not. Support means acting as if they were in agreement. Make this a cultural mindset. |
| | Negative result from decision. | No second-guessing. Adjust, problem-solve and move ahead. Never belabor the decision. |

The bottom line: understand the structure that works best for you. Assess your strengths and weaknesses, not just as they relate to aptitudes and education, but more importantly, those pertaining to attitudes and relationships.

## Success Factor 2. Fully Understand the Level of Responsibility Involved

Although responsibility doesn't seem to be a core value readily embraced these days, entrepreneurs have no choice. You not only have all the responsibility, but you had better embrace it with eyes wide open. You must learn how to handle the heightened commitment, stress and time challenges.

If we compare job positions to the medical profession, an employee is like an undergraduate still learning the names of bones, organs and anatomy. A department manager is in "medical school" learning about real-life challenges. An executive might parallel an intern being directly responsible for some actual "cases."

As an entrepreneur you face "brain surgery" every day. You get to make the hardest decisions and solve the toughest problems. When the business changes because of the economy, competition or technology, you have to figure out how to cope with that change.

Entrepreneurs typically reply, "I want to be my own boss, so sure, I know all that." Knowing when you're sick and when to take some medicine doesn't make you a doctor. Wanting to be the boss doesn't make you a successful entrepreneur capable of handling the added pressure. The following tips will help you cope with the heightened level of responsibility:

- Prioritize and rank problems/decisions — handle the most important things first.
- Delegate decisions and authority — don't second-guess; support and move on.
- Engage outside experts — don't try to do it all yourself.
- Create diversions and outlets — have some play time, but don't be fooled into thinking you can create total balance.

## Success Factor 3. Understand and Set Goals

Individuals considered successful, when asked why they believe they're successful, may talk about perseverance, hard work, even luck. Almost all have specific, measurable goals. Goal-setting processes usually include five characteristics. Goals need to be written, have specific outcomes, be realistic, have time parameters and be stated in positive terms. Another way to look at goals is the acronym SMART — as shown in the graphic. The only missing ingredient is the written requirement. Most goal-setting teachers say writing your goals down creates a contract, albeit an informal one. It solidifies the intention and keeps it visible, much like a daily or weekly to-do list.

It's important to remember goals are meant to guide you and create a powerful subconscious intention; they're not meant to create an absolute success or failure mindset. Goal setting, by the way, doesn't have to be the daunting task you may have envisioned. Here's a simple worksheet that may help.

## Goal-Setting Worksheet

All the goal-setting research and programs use essentially the same five rules for defining and pursuing goals. Goals must be realistic, time-specific, stated with a positive declaration, measurable and written.

Here's a worksheet you can use to develop and record any goal you want to accomplish. Start by writing a first draft (as you see it):

My goal is:_____

_____

Now go through the first four steps.

1. **Is your goal realistic, but challenging?**

   I can accomplish my goal because:

   _____

   _____

2. **Put a timeframe on it.**

   I will accomplish this goal by _____

3. **State the goal in a positive context.** State what you ARE going to do (or be). Don't use negative terms: "I'll have 5 employees" rather than "I will not hire more than 5 employees".

   _____

   _____

4. **State it in measurable terms or set up ways to measure it (dollars, steps completed).**

   Specifically I'll know my goal is accomplished when:

   _____

   _____

5. **Now write out your final, complete goal.**

   My goal is:

   _____

   _____

## Success Factor 4. Establish Steadfast Values Inside Your Business

Compromises are necessary in business. We often bend rules to accommodate a special order or our favorite (and most profitable) customer. There can be, however, no compromise regarding the values and principles upon which you've established your business. Here are some core values that you can turn into business principles. Once you define your values and principles, you'll need to develop policies around them.

**Honesty.** Is your value about fairness, integrity or openness? A business principle might be "All dealings with prospects, customers and employees will be direct, honest and fair."

**Respect for others.** Perhaps the golden rule is the principle here.

**Work ethic.** A good principle involving work ethic is "We work hard and we play hard." Policies around effort and dedication to customer support may be germane.

Although sound financial practices are needed in any business, instilling a core value around money can be counter-productive. Past economic adversity can lead to "penny-wise and dollar-foolish" decisions. Affluent backgrounds, on the other hand, may produce overly cautious or frivolous financial outcomes, depending on how the affluence was created.

Likewise, social, spiritual or religious values are generally only appropriate as core principles for a business whose product or service is related to those values.

Once you define your core values and develop policies around those values, you must do two things.

1. Make the message part of everything you do and say — advertising, employee handbook, training materials, support and service procedures, etc.

2. Empower employees with the authority to act and with unquestioned support.

Instill your values in your business and employees. Ensure they are never misplaced or compromised.

## Success Factor 5. Get and Keep the Right Attitude

If you think you can or can't, you're right! Henry Ford is credited with that statement. You've probably, at one time or another, uttered the phrase "he has a bad attitude," referring to someone who is complaining or exhibiting other negative characteristics. Hopefully, you've often thought or said "I like his attitude," when witnessing positive actions. Attitude, positive or negative, has a huge impact on the success of a business. It's contagious, affecting people you encounter as well as your own ability to function.

Business owners and managers must set the stage for a positive environment. It's much easier to create and sustain an upbeat setting than it is to continually neutralize negative actions. Another challenge is dealing swiftly and positively with inevitable problems. You can meet both challenges by:
- Posting positive reinforcement messages
- Exhibiting the kind of behavior you want from others
- Rewarding positive outcomes. No, it doesn't always need to be monetary
- Complimenting every positive action openly and enthusiastically

## Summary

Ask business owners why they are, or are not, successful and those feeling good may attribute their success to marketing, location or product superiority. When you find out how they run their business, you'll see a connection to at least three of the factors outlined in this chapter. On the other hand, those citing bad luck or describing how they "ran out of money" or the "timing was bad" will have little, if any, link to the factors described. They will probably have no written goals, difficulty in describing what they stand for, a poor outlook (attitude), and likely are in the wrong structure for their personality.

## CASE STUDY
## Building a Successful B2B Software Company

**The Company.** Excalibur is a B2B software firm created for the exclusive purpose of developing an oil & gas industry software package. The creation incorporated the success factors outlined in this chapter.

**The Challenge.** In 1980, the oil & gas industry (O&G) was booming. O&G independents were exploring, drilling and making money. They had, at best, poor computer systems to track investors, payouts, expenses and general accounting.

**The Client.** An O&G executive and former client (Mr. A) sold an O&G investment company and started an exploration company (API).

**The Journey and the Discovery.** Mr. A contacted this author about replacing their limited, outsourced computer service with an in-house solution. This was a great opportunity to build a software solution that could be marketed to other O&G companies. Mr. A agreed to pay the development costs in return for a royalty (something common in the O&G industry) on future sales of the software.

**The Solution.** A partner was added to the company who could put together a marketing plan while the author focused on creating the software. We launched Excalibur and proceeded to implement the software for API. At the same time, we embarked on creating a B2B marketing plan. Within three years, Excalibur had forty employees in three offices. The factors discussed in this article were an integral part of Excalibur's success.

## Conclusion

**Know your entrepreneurial personality.** At the time, this author did not understand that "The Painless Partner" was the best organizational structure for me. In order to build a viable company, we needed solid sales and marketing talent. Past experience led to hiring a person who also would be an owner. Excalibur grew because decision making was explicit and partners (others were added along the way) always supported each other, whether a decision proved successful or not. The structure fit the entrepreneurial personalities hired.

**Fully understand the level of responsibility involved.** The partners often worked or met after normal business hours. "Homework" was common as well. Yet, each made time for family, social and recreational activities. Every partner knew there was no such thing as total work/life "balance," but also knew that trying for balance was necessary to set an example for the employees. The partners understood the responsibility of making sure employees maintained outside interests for the success of the organization.

**Understand and set goals.** The partners were students of various self-help gurus — Zig Ziglar, Denis Waitley, Wayne Dyer and others — and knew that setting goals, writing them down and putting a timeframe on them, was important. The process was kept simple by using tools similar to the worksheet included in this chapter.

Establish steadfast values inside your business. Sticking to our original values turned out to be one of the most important factors in Excalibur's success. Two principles were unwavering: the quality of the product and listening to the clients. Standards were established for every piece of code, documentation and testing. As to clients, it wasn't just about providing good customer service. Customer input was actively sought and acted upon. Customers knew the company would follow up on requested software enhancements. The owners instilled that value in all employees, processes, service procedures and marketing collateral.

**Get and keep the right attitude.** Again, Ziglar, Waitley, Dyer and others were a great influence. Negative influences were not allowed to pervade this business world. There were times when problems seemed to outnumber and overshadow solutions. Then positive messages were posted and a "we can overcome any problem" attitude was instilled throughout the organization. The owners set the tone. We rewarded positive behavior frequently and openly. We developed a more productive workforce by creating an environment where people were not afraid to have fun and be themselves.

Excalibur survived the tough 1980s oil recession and well into the 1990s. API recovered all of its development costs through software sale royalties. Excalibur was sold in 1998 but the product is still being used today. The company would never have accomplished what it did without a strong influence from the Five Success Factors for Entrepreneurs.

**Larry Brummond**, president of The Write Touch Inc., is a freelance B2B business writer, speaker and entrepreneur coach/mentor. His business career includes a decade as president and co-founder of Excalibur, a successful oil and gas software company. In addition to 25 years in the software business, Larry's background includes business brokering, finance and insurance, training and management consulting. Larry writes business communications for B2B marketing, operations, and business development. He has a bachelor's degree in management from the University of Phoenix, is an Advanced Toastmaster and has been a member of BMA Colorado since 2009.

# DEVELOPING
# CONTENT

ADVICE FROM THE TOP

# 8 | A Roadmap for Conversion-Driven Marketing

## Targeting Informational Offers to B2B Buyers

Sam Eidson

In the last decade B2B marketing has evolved significantly, and the pace of change is increasing. While that makes the future hard to predict, at 90octane we believe that within our working lives we will see an end to separate marketing and sales departments. Some organizations are expediting the process by closing the gap between marketing and sales through an approach called conversion-driven marketing.

This style of marketing creates a shift from hard-sell, mass communication promotions to measurable, targeted marketing that facilitates the prospect's decision-making process and sets the foundation for a valuable relationship. Implemented properly, conversion-driven marketing creates accountability and transparency between marketing and sales.

In this chapter, we briefly outline the steps to set up a successful conversion-driven marketing program. We then go in-depth into a methodology for presenting informational offers to target audiences to facilitate complex B2B sales.

## Steps to a Successful Program

### Readiness Stage

While the conversion-driven approach can be applied to different types of campaigns, a common objective is to deliver qualified leads to a sales force. If this is the goal, make sure the organization is ready. The most important step is bringing marketing and sales together. Ideally, a champion from the sales leadership will join the marketing steering committee to bring customer insight, establish lead goals, and gain buy-in to ensure the sales force follows up and reports back on lead status.

As sales and marketing determine program requirements, the infrastructure can be developed. First, decide on tools: will your organization require the implementation of complete marketing automation and sales force automation systems from the start, or can you ease into these? Identify the processes that need to be in place to close the loop.

It is critical to establish open communication during the Readiness Stage. Develop pre-campaign communications to ensure the entire organization sees what is coming and put clear results reporting in place to create as much transparency as possible.

> *"It is critical to establish open communication during the Readiness Stage."*

## Goals and Success Metrics

In setting goals and success metrics, start with the end in mind. Identify the specific growth goals then draw a direct line between these goals and the metrics that will tell you whether you are on track. Ensure these metrics can actually be tracked. Set up regular, efficient reporting cycles to analyze and optimize tactics.

## Purchase Process and Offer Map

Starting with a customer who is representative of your target market, map out the purchase process for your product or service. Identify the roles that are included in that decision. From there, informational offers can be mapped to the purchase process, using the method described in detail in the next section.

## Lead Nurturing and Scoring

If the purchase process is short and appropriate for a broad audience, immediately passing leads to the sales force may be sufficient. For a longer, considered sale with a narrower target, lead nurturing is advisable. This means creating a multi-touch marketing campaign to learn more about a raw lead so you can qualify them. It involves giving prospects more opportunities to view and respond to your organization's informational offers before being contacted by a sales representative. The most efficient way to achieve this is by incorporating a marketing automation system. Coupled with the lead-nurturing process, you should develop a lead-scoring method identifying what explicit (profile-based) criteria and implicit (behavior- and interaction-based) criteria constitute a qualified lead.

## Execution and Optimization

Finally, create the nuts and bolts of the campaign including creative strategy, media planning, asset development and technical planning to incorporate tracking of the success metrics identified in the strategy. Once the program launches, follow your measurement plan to gauge the program on its key success metrics and optimization.

# Offer Map

As you create a program, the Offer Map merits special attention as it is one of the most critical components of a conversion-driven marketing program. A good informational offer placed in front of the right prospect at the right time will entice the individual to provide his information, brand your organization as a thought leader that is on the customer's team, and warm up an otherwise cold sales call.

To develop an effective Offer Map, start by analyzing the target audience. Demographics and psychographics will help with target messaging and creative. For offers, add a careful analysis of how the prospect organization makes its collective decision.

## Identify the Individuals

First, bring the company to the individual level. Once you have identified the segments of organizations you are targeting, identify the titles of the individuals in those organizations who contribute to the purchase decision and the roles they play in the process.

As in any marketing process, this requires research. Use a combination of online listening and traditional qualitative research. Starting with the right prospects will help keep the findings relevant, even if you are working with very few data points. Work under the inaccurate but directionally correct premise that your research is representative of your entire market. In reality, this helps you target the most promising prospects.

## Detail the Purchase Process and Roles

Next, identify each individual's role in the purchase decision. The completed picture should look something like this:

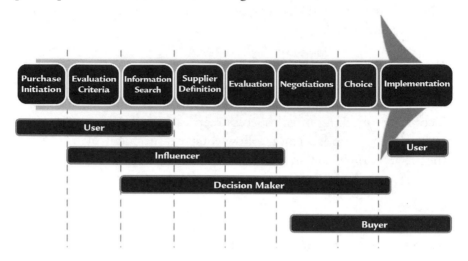

Of course, your version will be less generic. While envisioning a representative target company, replace the term "User" with the title of the individual who would be hands-on with your solution. Technical assistants, customer service representatives and programmer/developers are examples. In a midsize or large organization, these people don't decide what equipment or services the company will purchase for their use, but they use them day in and day out. They have the most knowledge about the incumbent solutions' fit, strengths and weaknesses — and the inefficiencies the weaknesses are causing. They may also have ideas about competitive advantage lost by not overcoming these weaknesses.

However, barriers keep this information from surfacing: the user is too "in the weeds" to realize there is a problem with the status quo; he may even fear that solving the problem will endanger his job. That's where the next role in the process takes place.

A good manager will recognize the problem, work with the user to quantify the problem and gain consensus on working toward a solution. This manager is sometimes the decision maker and sometimes an influencer reporting to the decision maker. A buyer may come in at the end of the process to negotiate price, seal the deal and set future purchases in motion.

This is one picture of how conversion marketing can work, but it is critical to remember there is no standard process or set of roles. The purchase-process graphic starts with "Purchase Initiation," but the description in the previous paragraph starts at least one phase back with "Recognize there is a problem." Use primary research within your organization and channel partners to identify what your purchase process looks like.

## Add the Positioning Overlay

Once the purchase process and roles are mapped, think of the central questions each influential user has in the phases where they have a major role. If your organization could give one clear response to that question, what would it be? By developing a simple matrix overlaying the roles and phases, you come up with something like this:

| **User:** "I have a problem." | **User:** "My need has specific requirements." | **Influencer:** "Is it a technical fit?" | **Buyer:** "What will it cost (in all) and when will I see a return?" | **Decision Maker:** "Will you evolve with our industry?" | **Buyer:** "How do I buy?" |
|---|---|---|---|---|---|
| **Business:** "We have helped customers with similar problems." | **Business:** "We meet the specs." | **Business:** "Yes" (Or "No") | **Business:** "In less than 1.5 years you will see a return on your purchase." | **Business:** "We are thought leaders and committed to this vertical." | **Business:** "We have a network of distributors around the U.S." |

## Identify and Place the Informational Offers

Now you are ready to plan your informational offers. The types of informational offers are practically unlimited. Examples include white papers, webinars, educational videos, ROI calculators, spec sheets, and even simple content on a Web page. Deciding on a type and format can be a very detailed process, but here are some best practices:

- Select a format that fits the target audience's habits for digesting information.
- Think of the offer's placement. Will it be presented on a Web page, through a print piece, via e-mail or some other way?
- Consider editing a piece that is already available. Creating offers is one of the most time-consuming parts of a lead-generation program. But also make sure the quality of information is the highest

possible since this is also one of the most important parts of a lead-generation program.

• Plan for the offer's role in the lead-generation and nurturing process. At the end of the day you want a qualified lead: a prospect with enough qualifying information to send him to a sales representative. Your lead-generation and nurturing process needs to be set up to capture both profile data — through forms or surveys — and behavioral data — by tracking what types of content the user views and how he reacts to marketing materials. Some offers will be worthy of placing behind a registration form; others won't. Most online offers can be linked to tracking mechanisms allowing you to learn something about the prospect's behavior.

Adding the informational offers to the most important buying phases completes the Offer Map. In the example provided, the marketer has determined that the essential phases for the organization's differentiation are "I have a problem," "What will my total cost and payback be?" and "Will you evolve with our industry?" To demonstrate the organization's positioning in each phase, he has overlaid a case study, ROI calculator and webinar in the appropriate phases.

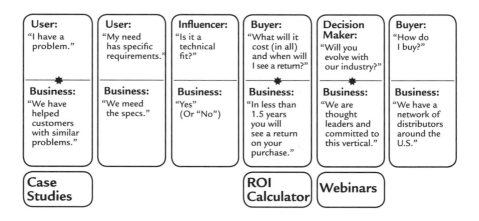

At this point, the marketer is ready to develop the informational offers and develop the media, creative and lead-nurturing plans to put them in front of the right prospect at the right time.

## CASE STUDY
## Gates Corporation — Generating Qualified
## B2B Sales Leads

**The Client.** For the past nine years, 90octane has partnered with Gates Corporation — a leading industrial and automotive belt and hose manufacturer — on an increasingly in-depth conversion-driven marketing program. The result has been a move from push-oriented and attribute-focused marketing to measurable, two-way communication with prospects. The company's strategic demand-generation programs put fast, accurate and high-quality prospects into the hands of Gates sales teams, building relationships based on trust and creating prime sales opportunities.

**The Journey.** Prior to 2001, Gates was relying on attribute-focused trade advertising that left room for improvement as far as cost per lead, and sales results were not linked to specific marketing sources. 90octane partnered with the manufacturer to add measurable, response-driven marketing to the Gates marketing mix. The first campaign efforts included e-mails to the company's house list, white papers that prospects are motivated to download and online tools that helped engineers create designs with Gates products. With initially promising results, the program grew and the tactics became more sophisticated. Currently, each of the three Gates business units has its own program. Tactics range from webinars to cost savings calculators to Web expos (online tradeshows), and sales results are attributed back to specific marketing tactics.

**The Implementation.** At the outset of each program, the marketing team pinpoints the target audience (often comprised of either original equipment manufacturers or maintenance and repair organizations), strategizes how to reach them, and sets measurable goals. Marketing and sales representatives mutually agree on what defines a qualified, sales-ready lead. Response-driven tactics such as e-mail, search engine optimization, paid search advertising, online media, vertical search and social media help point prospects to campaign-specific landing pages and microsites where they register for and download targeted offers. These offers are tailored to prospects at different stages of the purchase process — such as awareness, research, evaluation and decision making.

For example, the program might target line engineers and plant managers who need to know that their plant's downtime for roller chain changeovers is unnecessary and that a better solution exists. Solutions, such as synchronous belt drives, are presented through white papers, cost savings calculators, webinars, Web expos, paid search and push advertising. These efforts are integrated with trade advertising and PR.

Offer Mapping to the purchase process is used to improve targeting, media planning and lead qualification. Low involvement offers like Belt Tips — brief weekly e-mails containing power transmission best practices — are used at the beginning of a nurture process, and they feed into higher-involvement informational offers that are specific to a Gates solution. Users' purchase stages are measured by their engagement in early stage offers (e.g., white papers) to later stage offers (e.g., catalogs and distributor look-ups). Only when leads are deemed qualified, based on their registration profiles and behavior, are they passed to the Gates sales team and distributors.

**The Results.** Tracking the entire marketing and sales process creates a bridge to quantify sales success against marketing investment, and the team can zero in on areas of improvement for future campaigns. Gates sees over 1,500 leads per month, and the media cost per lead has dropped 94 percent. Profile and behavior qualification data are passed to sales to help them close deals. The link between marketing campaigns and sales results is now being made, and the data are being used to determine program ROI, optimize the program, and improve the partnership between marketing, sales and distributors.

**Sam Eidson** is a founding partner of 90octane, a conversion-driven marketing agency specializing in B2B lead generation, B2C demand generation and nonprofit donor acquisition. Sam earned his bachelor's degree in international relations from Brown University and his MBA from Darden School of Business, University of Virginia. With over 17 years of experience in interactive marketing, integrated marketing strategy and management consulting, Sam has delivered presentations at the 2006 National BMA Conference, at local BMA chapter events and at the 2010 Integrated Marketing Summit in Denver. He has been an active member of BMA Colorado since 2001.

# 9 | Mastering Persuasive B2B Sales Writing Techniques

Casey Demchak

There's really no getting around it. There's the kind of writing you did to please your English teacher, and there's the kind of writing you do to motivate prospects to buy products. And they're two completely different styles of writing. Many B2B marketing professionals have competent writing skills, but they don't know the secret techniques for writing persuasive marketing communication materials.

Does this challenge sound familiar to you? Not only does good sales copy have to be compelling, it also needs to grab prospects and motivate them to take action. Meeting this demand can be intimidating, especially in the B2B market.

Why? Because clever headlines, zippy one-liners and images of good-looking people standing next to your products aren't going to sell them. Put simply, fluff doesn't work with B2B. What does work is strong, engaging sales copy that's backed by sound communication strategies.

Fortunately, writing persuasive B2B sales copy is about to become a much easier task. This chapter includes a series of techniques that will help you get the attention of your prospects and inspire them to buy your products. In this chapter you'll learn specific strategies for writing B2B sales copy that engages prospects and motivates them to buy your product or service.

## Four Basic Tips to Get You Started

Before getting into the specific building blocks of strong sales writing, there are four "overview" tips that can be applied to all your B2B marketing materials.

## 1. Pick the Voice That's Right for You

One of the biggest mistakes in sales writing is copy that is not written in the right conversational style. It's either too stiff and formal or too overblown with hype.

All of your sales copy should have a common and consistent conversational tone throughout your marketing campaign. Don't think of your writing as words on paper, think of it as your campaign's voice and personality. After you choose the appropriate voice, write all your campaign materials in this conversational style.

## 2. Use Simple Words and Short Sentences

The quickest way to kill good sales copy is to use long-winded sentences that are loaded with punctuation and four-syllable words. Using short sentences gives each of your thoughts its own individual stage, and it makes it easy for busy prospects to read and digest your copy quickly.

## 3. Make Your Copy Fast and Easy to Read

Marketing copy that's intended to sell should be written in a concise style, and be formatted so it looks inviting to the eye. Here is a simple three-step formula that will help you accomplish this.

- Break your copy up with tight subheads that tout product benefits.
- Limit your descriptive paragraphs to three or four lines and then start another paragraph.
- Use sharp, action-oriented bullet points to highlight product benefits and create open white space in your copy.

## 4. Write Believable Copy

When attempting to be persuasive with your B2B sales copy, don't make the mistake of going too far with sizzle and hype. Always assume your audience is intelligent and skeptical.

Make sure every word you write really means something. If you write fluff for the sake of fluff, your audience will see right through it. And once you've

planted a seed of distrust in your audience, they'll never trust you again. The example on the previous page shows how to write easy-to-read copy that clearly communicates product benefits without a lot of added hype.

## The Building Blocks of Persuasive Sales Writing

### Start With a Strategic Headline

The easiest way to improve any collateral marketing piece is to create a better headline. The two goals of every headline are to engage your prospects and to compel them to read your body copy. Here is a quick tip that will help you accomplish this: *Use simple, benefit-driven headlines.*

> *"The easiest way to improve any collateral marketing piece is to create a better headline."*

Many people waste a lot of time trying to come up with headlines that are witty, zippy or clever when something straight-forward and simple may be the better choice — especially in B2B sales copy. Consider these three headline examples:

- *How to increase office productivity and reduce health care costs*
- *Five steps to cutting health care costs by 30 percent*
- *Want to lower your company's health care costs by 30 percent?*

Clever, witty or zippy? Hardly. But, if these three headlines were directed at human resource directors they would arouse interest, get attention and, most likely, motivate them to read the copy underneath. Why? Because each headline states or implies a benefit. And it's strongly implied that how to realize the benefit being promised will be revealed in the body copy below the headline.

### Show Your Prospects You Feel Their Pain

A common mistake when writing sales copy is to begin by touting your product's features and benefits. A better course of action is to start by showing you have an understanding of your prospects' challenges. This approach makes your copy more about them and less about you. It also gives you the credibility to then position your product as a solution to their challenges.

## Example:

*You're not asking for much. You just want to shorten your selling cycle, increase sales, and gain greater competitive share. Oh, and you'd prefer a solution that's customized to meet your needs while serving as a profitable revenue stream.*

*The answer is a flexible leasing program from Jones Equipment Finance. And I can tailor one to specifically benefit you, your dealer, and your customers.*

> **"A common mistake when writing sales copy is to begin by touting your product's features and benefits."**

## Focus on Benefits

Focusing strictly on product features, instead of product benefits, is a common mistake many writers make when creating B2B sales copy. Benefits are the "yeah, so-what's-in-it-for-me" aspect of a product, and it's what your prospects care about the most. When you write about your product's features, be sure to immediately follow up with the corresponding benefit.

## Example:
**The WaterRich Excel System**

*Its open system (**feature**) allows you to implement any protocol required for prescribed treatments (**benefit**). Our industry-leading Water-K software (**feature**) enables you to create protocols that match individual patient requirements (**benefit**).*

*In addition, the WaterRich Excel System includes a highly-intuitive user interface and ergonomic handling (**features**) for greater ease of use (**benefit**). Its well-balanced components (**feature**) make therapies easier to perform (**benefit**) which enhances patient safety (**benefit**).*

## Use "Action" Bullet Points

A great way to communicate product benefits is through sharp, concise bullet points that begin with dynamic action words.

## Example:

Through our direct mail programs, Jimstone Marketing can:
- *Develop leading-edge marketing messages for your business.*
- *Build your brand reputation with prospects.*
- *Drive more patients into your facility.*
- *Fuel your bottom line and grow your practice.*

## Offer Proof Through Belief Builders

After you have effectively communicated your product benefits, it's time to offer a little proof to back up your marketing claims. Whenever possible, include as many "belief builders" as you can into your sales copy. Belief builders are pieces of proof that support your primary marketing claims. A list of basic belief builders includes:

- Charts and graphs
- Published statistics
- Testimonials from respected third-party experts
- Case study quotations

## Create Limited-Time Special Offers

Nearly every successful sales piece is built around a special offer. The most effective special offers are those that have built-in time limits.

The reasoning is simple. Setting a time limit on your offer motivates prospects to act sooner rather than later. Also, including a free special report or a free tip sheet with your limited-time offer will further motivate prospects to act.

### Example:

*Order by April 1, 2010, and receive a 20 percent discount off our standard price. Plus, we'll also send you a **free** tip sheet on how to increase your sales leads by 15 percent or more.*

## Reverse the Risk

Limited-time discounts, special offers and free giveaways are great — but they are not always enough to motivate your prospects to take action.

One more thing you can do to persuade them is to reverse the risk on your special offer. An easy way to do this is to offer prospects a 30-day trial or a guarantee of some kind.

Reversing the risk essentially means your prospects have nothing to lose because they can always get their money back. This takes the risk off them and puts it on you, which can further motivate customers to act.

## Make a Strong Call to Action

Always tell prospects the next definite step you want them to take in the buying process. This is very easy to do with call-to-action lines. Never be passive when writing call-to-action lines. Always be confident, straightforward and direct.

## Examples:

*Don't Delay! Call Us Today At (800) 555-XXXX*
*Take Advantage of This Special Low Price — Call Today!*
*For More Information, Call Us Right Now At (800) 555-XXXX*

## Three Easy Ways to Fine-Tune Your Persuasive Sales Writing

There are three inside secrets that can really fine-tune your sales writing.

### 1. Don't be Afraid to use the Fear Factor

People worry a lot. They fear being left behind, not being up-to-date, and they fear not having the latest tools they need to compete. Take advantage of this.

Read and listen to successful B2B marketing campaigns and you'll find them peppered with certain phrases: "Can you really afford to know less than your competitor?" "Your competitor isn't loyal to yesterday's technology standards. Why are you?"

Although subtle, fear is utilized in almost every winning campaign. You can inject fear into your campaign simply by suggesting to prospects the consequences they may face if they don't buy your product.

### 2. Create Value Demonstrations

This is a technique you can use to put the price of your product in perspective. Your goal with a value demonstration is to clearly explain how your product pays for itself.

### Example:

*Our DVD, "How To Generate Twice As Many B2B Leads In Half The Time," is loaded with hundreds of essential lead-generating secrets. At only $24.95, you're probably paying less than a dime for every tip that could fuel the growth of your business.*

### 3. Stress Emotional Benefits

Most products have emotional benefits that are often overlooked. For example, intraocular lenses used in cataract surgery may help restore the vision of elderly people suffering from cataracts. The lens may also be highly biocompatible with the eye, promoting quicker recovery times following surgery.

But don't forget the emotional benefits of such a product. Restoring elderly people's vision gives them hope, makes them feel young, and allows them to experience the joy of watching their grandchildren play. It may also make them feel more vibrant and alive.

Most products have important emotional benefits for users. Remember to consider them when writing your next marketing campaign.

There you have it. A nice set of persuasive sales writing techniques that can help you motivate your prospects to reach for their wallets and buy your products. Remember, getting prospects to take action isn't about being zippy, witty or clever. It's all about using proven sales writing techniques that are backed by sound strategies.

## CASE STUDY
## Ubiquity Group

**The Challenge.** Lisa Herter, President and CEO of Ubiquity Group, faced a unique B2B marketing situation. She had to create a marketing campaign for a large medical device company that educated nephrologists about the benefits of Continual Renal Replacement Therapy (CRRT) as a means of treating acute kidney injury patients.

The challenge was to create awareness about a therapy, not directly sell a device. All marketing messages had to be supported with clinical evidence that proved CRRT is a valid therapy for acute kidney injury patients with the goal being that this evidence would, down the road, sell CRRT treatment devices.

"Nephrologists are really interested in information that comes from factual data and clinical evidence," said Lisa. "So it was important that we tied our messaging around clinical data, and delivered it in the proper voice and style."

**The Client.** Ubiquity is a marketing firm that specializes in generating demand for medical device companies. They help companies generate more awareness, product demand, and in turn — greater revenue.

**The Journey.** "We did a lot of research on nephrologists, specifically looking at their communication preferences, and we developed personas in order to craft marketing messages," reported Lisa. "Based on our research, we were able to determine that messaging based on clinical evidence and physician-benefit statements would have a higher success rate than traditional or patient-benefit messaging."

**The Discovery.** Lisa Herter and her team at Ubiquity concluded nephrologists would spend a very limited time reading any marketing materials related to a CRRT awareness campaign because they were quite comfortable with existing treatment modalities.

"Given that we had to move nephrologists to action using very few words, we knew we couldn't use a general everyday writing style," reported Lisa. "We decided to employ persuasive copywriting techniques that would stress the benefits of CRRT, support our marketing statements with belief builders, and motivate nephrologists to download white papers and sign up for webinars."

**The Solution.** Print ads, Web copy and e-blasts all featured headlines and subheads that were based on facts pulled from clinical trials and published articles. All of the heads and subheads were concise and communicated important benefits related to using CRRT as a modality for treating acute kidney injury.

Secondary benefits were communicated through sharp, action-oriented bullet points. Descriptive sales-copy paragraphs were limited to just a few lines each. The use of benefit-driven headlines, action-oriented bullet points, and very short paragraphs created marketing pieces that had a very open and easy-to-read look.

"We also employed confident, strong call-to-action lines," said Lisa Herter. "If nephrologists only quickly glanced at our copy, we wanted them to get an immediate benefit message, and we accomplished that using all of these techniques."

**The Implementation.** To assure the campaign's persuasive sales message was consistent and accurate, we developed a key message copy platform, which is an internal document that included all of the approved marketing copy for the campaign. It was used as a springboard for writing the campaign's print ads, e-blasts and Web pages.

By serving as a home for all approved marketing messages, the key message copy platform made it easier to write a body of consistent, persuasive marketing materials that had a uniformed voice and message. This was a much more effective strategy than recreating our messaging as we developed each new marketing piece.

**The Results.** Lisa Herter reports that the persuasive sales writing techniques employed in their client's CRRT awareness campaign have been a success. As a key part of the campaign, a new microsite (www.crrtcounts.com) was launched in October of 2009.

Web-based ads and print ads ran for six months with call-to-action lines directed to specific landing pages that made it easy to track from which trade publications and Web ads visitors came. The most surprising statistic was the 102 unique visits to the website from six print publications.

Call-to-action lines motivating nephrologists to download white papers have also been a success. As of December 2010 the white papers download page at crrtcounts.com showed 1,124 views, which accounted for 19 percent of total page views.

In addition, campaign call-to-action lines asking physicians to sign up for webinars have resulted in 1,851 page views, or 31 percent of the total pages viewed on the site.

"It's harder in B2B to measure ROI specifically because product doesn't fly off the shelves," says Lisa. "But our goal was to build greater awareness for CRRT that could affect sales not just today, but a year down the road as well. Through the persuasive sales writing techniques we employed in this campaign, we went a long way towards achieving that goal."

**Casey Demchak** is an expert in writing high-impact B2B marketing communication materials. He is the author of the book, *Essential Sales Writing Secrets*, and he has published several special reports and trade journal articles in various publications. He also hosted the VoiceAmerica™ Business Internet radio talk show, "Essential Marketing Secrets." Casey has been a member of the Business Marketing Association, Colorado chapter, since 2003.

# 10 Why Value-Based Content Is King

Marian Robinson

**M**arketing as a discipline changes as rapidly as technology. Marketing plans, and the content that is developed to achieve them, change in response to new technologies, new means of communication and the changing sophistication of our audiences. Business marketing presents its own unique challenges. The rules that we must abide by, the roles of our audiences, and the restrictions under which we must operate tend to be more complex than those of our consumer-marketing colleagues. Regardless of the type of marketing you practice, the content of your marketing messaging is critical to the success of your work. Here's how to ensure that your content reigns.

## What You Know Is WRONG!

Chances are your marketing materials will provide readers with the classic in B2B marketing — features and benefits messaging. Most professional marketers have been classically schooled in differentiating their products this way. As a result, most marketing collateral provides an exhaustive list of things the products have (features) and what those things do (benefits). Not that there's anything wrong with that.

---

Typical *Features* and **Benefits** Copy

*Barcode verification* **ensures right source ingredients**

*Setup Wizard* **makes installation easy**

*High-speed fluid delivery* **reduces the time to fill a bag**

*Air and occlusion detection* **prevents delivery inaccuracies**

---

But, it's the wrong way to sell a product.[1] Why, then, does every marketing textbook focus on features and benefits?

## What Do Customers Want?

To answer that question, let's start with what they *don't* want. Customers *don't* want to be "sold." (Bought a used car lately?) What they *do* want is to solve a problem: their problem. They want to do something better, faster, cheaper, or simply improve on a current process.

Your dizzying array of product features and benefits *may* provide your customers with some insight into what your product does. It may provide customers with some ideas as to how they might use your product. But it isn't likely that your customers can determine from your current marketing messages just exactly *how* your product solves their problems. Right?

As you can see, the typical approach puts the entire burden on the customer to decipher how those features and benefits might address the problem or problems they're looking to solve. Your job as a marketer is to understand your customers' challenges well enough to understand their challenges in getting clear marketing content. Once you have that understanding, you can use it to deliver impactful marketing messaging: messaging that sells.

Can your readers clearly identify what's remarkable about your product in your messaging? Are you sure? No doubt you have a plethora of marketing materials deployed for your product — brochures, websites, direct mail, newsletters, customer letters, training materials, microsites, landing pages, presentations, videos and more. While each is designed for different impact, is the messaging consistent? Is it clear? Are you remarkable? Is your product the ONLY answer?

The answer to these questions is your products' differentiation. We all understand the *power* of differentiation in product marketing.[2] Numerous books and articles have discussed the need to provide customers with a clear answer as to why your product is unique among its competitors. Now you need to find a remarkable way to communicate that clarity to give your messaging a distinct sales advantage.

## Advantages Sell

Once you have an understanding of what customers need, and the answers to why your product is unique, you can use that information to communicate its value to your customers. For customers, the "value proposition" is an amalgam of four factors.

1. **Business condition** — the problem(s) that keeps the customer up at night. What is it that causes your customer stress or puts the pressure on him? These are often key beliefs that your customer and/or his organization holds.

2. **Product advantages** — what your product does that alleviates the customer's pain or reduces the identified business condition(s). This answers the WIIFM (what's in it for me) from your customer's point of view.

3. **Product features** — what specifically your product has or does that solves the customer's pain.

4. **Customer value** — the answers to the above factors that create a story about the value of your product in your customer's mind.

If this sounds easy, it's not. But this kind of marketing messaging resonates with your sales team and their customers, and creates the kinds of wins that will make you a marketing guru.

---

Example of Advantage Messaging:

## Key Belief/Business Condition

Compliance/need to comply with Joint Commission requirements and guidelines for hospital accreditation. Need to have accreditation for reimbursement (Centers for Medicare and Medicaid Services). Anxiety Question: What would be the business impact if you failed to comply during a Joint Commission inspection of your facility?

## Product Advantage(s)

Demonstrate compliance to Joint Commission Medication Management Standards during an inspection.

## Product Feature

Automated formulary reports that comply with the Medication Management Standards.

## Customer Value

Eliminate fear of job loss or repercussions from a failed Joint Commission inspection.

All of this gets communicated in your marketing messaging, and gets summarized in an advantage statement. For example: *The only system that complies with Joint Commission Medication Management Standards.*

---

Just remember, the messaging that you've identified isn't an advantage if it's required by law or by the industry, or if everyone else has it. It's just a "check-box" item. For example, many medical device manufacturers will pound their chests over their regulatory compliance, FDA registration or CE (Conformité Européene). Yet they can't sell their products in the U.S. and European markets without that regulatory compliance, and neither can anyone else. Check the box.

So how can you test your advantages? A checklist is helpful:

✓ Your advantage must be true. Maybe consumer marketing can get away with hyperbole and false claims, but that's not true in B2B.

✓ Your advantage must be measured against something — your competition or another way for the customer to solve the problem.

✓ Your advantage must be clear to your customers. "Friendly" customer service is not clear or quantifiable.

✓ Your advantage should be measurable (20 times faster than the competition), and meaningful (i.e., 24-hour service, if offered by everyone, is not meaningful).

✓ Your advantage should speak from the customer's viewpoint (reduces your training time by two hours).

Once crafted, your advantage messaging must help your customers understand how your product impacts them and leads them to the value that your product offers.

Getting to good advantage messaging is not as simple as rewriting your current features and benefits statements. Those statements support your advantage messaging and are different from it. Developing a knack for creating strong, value-packed advantage messaging requires working through the four factors to provide the backdrop, then creating the perfect punch line.

---

### Advantage Messaging Examples*

Good — Higher reduction in medication errors
*Better — 20% error reduction within 30 days*
Good — Broadest range of sizes
*Better — 50% more choices*
Good — Easier to install
*Better — Two hours less installation time*

*Keeping in mind the checklist above, and recognizing that body copy must provide the evidence for the messaging claims.

---

With advantage messaging, practice makes perfect. Create a worksheet using the four factors, then run your messaging through the checklist. Do a "gut check." Are your messages compelling? Are they believable? Is their value real to the customer? Once your messaging really speaks the language of your customers, you can move on to turning those advantages to sales.

## Advantage Messaging Worksheet

Notes on Key Beliefs/Business Conditions
- Customer values or beliefs
- Market drivers or business climate
- Economic issues
- Competitive challenges

Thoughts on Product Advantage(s)
- What does your product do uniquely well?
- How does that impact the customer's business condition or problem?

_____

_____

_____

_____

What Product Features differentiate you from the competition?

_____

_____

_____

How does that provide Customer Value?

_____

_____

_____

Final "Gut Check"

_____

_____

_____

_____

# How to Answer "Why buy?"

Now that you've got your messaging geared to your customer's needs, you need to answer the question, "Why buy **my** product?" One key way is to demonstrate it. Show your potential customers, live and in person, how your product can make a real difference in their day-to-day life. Use your demonstration to reinforce why your product is a better choice or — if you're lucky — the ONLY choice. And, be creative. Create a Web tool or a YouTube video. Have a sample product shipped to their home or office. If you sell a service, let your customers experience it before they buy. Offer enticements, discounts — whatever it takes to allow your customers to experience how your product's advantages enhance their lives.

## CASE STUDY
## Using Customer Advantages to Our Advantage

**The Challenge.** Baxa wanted to introduce a simple device for syringe infusion into a crowded marketplace. The issue was developing strong arguments for the use of this device in a market that already has a variety of competitive pumps/delivery systems and competing ready-to-use drugs that don't require this type of delivery system.

**The Client.** Key customers for the device are hospitals already using Baxa equipment to automate their syringe filling. The InFuse™ T10 Infuser is a simple and cost-effective means to administer those syringes to patients. Secondary customers are hospitals that use premix and are looking to reduce their overall drug costs or address their patients' clinical needs.

**The Journey.** The marketing department developed a traditional brochure and corresponding microsite to support the planned launch of the InFuse Infuser (Example 1). During the review process for the finished designs, Baxa determined that its usual features and benefits statements did not provide messaging compelling enough to get customers to change from their current practice — a key challenge for the success of the product launch.

---

### Example 1
### InFuse gives you time.

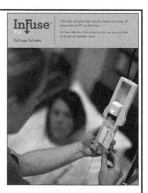

By taking over the work of slowly pushing intermittent antibiotics at the bedside, InFuse gives you time to focus on your patient. Simply load a Terumo 10 mL syringe into the infuser and activate.

Simple and durable, the InFuse Infuser requires no programming and setup is quick and easy. InFuse is compact, reliable, low-cost and easy to use.

- Simple to operate — no programming, one touch to activate
- Low cost — nominal acquisition price and minimal ongoing costs compared to programmable pumps
- Maintenance free — no batteries or calibration required
- Completely silent delivery — peace and quiet for you and your patients

---

**The Discovery.** Baxa product marketing has long employed differentiated messaging. The key shift in this case was moving to a customer-focused approach and crafting messaging that addressed the unique advantages that the InFuse provides for each of its identified audiences. Baxa then ensured that the messaging resonated in the copy and design of the marketing and sales collateral for the InFuse Infuser.

**The Solution.** "Do over." Using the process described, marketing team members stopped initial production and went through a painstaking analysis of the market, the customers and the industry drivers that affect how customers would perceive this product. All of the launch materials were rewritten (Example 2) and designs updated to reflect the new product advantage messaging.

---

### Example 2

**The *simple solution* for administration of non-rate-critical, intermittent IV antibiotics.**

**Reduces costs** — save up to **$3 per dose**, frees up smart pumps for critical infusions
**Simplifies administration** — requires no programming, one click to activate
**Eliminates maintenance** — simply wipe clean, no batteries or calibration required
**Improves patient experience** — helps prevent fluid overload, completely silent delivery

---

**The Implementation.** Deciding to start the collateral development over at the last minute raised some serious resource issues within the small in-house team. The rewriting and redesign process was disruptive to other scheduled projects. It also was frustrating for all of the reviewers and stakeholders to redo work that had previously been "completed." In addition, team members were under the gun to do great work in a hurry, as the planned product launch was in jeopardy, pending completion of the sales support materials.

**The Results.** While both difficult and costly in terms of employee time and effort, the updated product brochure tells a stronger "story" and provides more focused messaging to support the InFuse Infuser launch. All of the related marketing materials — the product microsite, sales training materials and promotional materials — were updated to reflect the new design and messaging. All of the sales collateral was well received by the sales team and the first product sale was achieved in about half the anticipated six- to nine-month sales cycle. In addition, the "customer advantage" approach has now been adopted across the board for sales and marketing materials, which is reflected in the projects that have been completed since spring 2010 when the company shifted to this new approach. To see the full example of the new InFuse Infuser launch materials, visit www.baxa.com/infuse.

## Conclusion

Writing good advantage messaging takes into account many of the axioms you have learned from other sources during your marketing career, such as focusing on the customer (WIIFM and "you can" vs. "we can" messaging) and differentiating your product. What your efforts hope to achieve is a clear message to your target audience around why you/ your product is a better choice. That choice needs to be based on the value that the customer feels you are providing and the pain or business condition that your product is impacting. Finally, your marketing messaging needs to communicate what you want your customers to know and what you want them to do once they know it.

---

[1] Author's note: for readability, products and services are referred to as "products" in most instances.

[2] Trout, Jack. *Differentiate or Die: Survival in Our Era of Killer Competition.* John Wiley & Sons Inc, 2000.

 **Marian Robinson's** professional career has included positions in technical writing, product management, corporate communications, politics and speechwriting, training consulting and quality assurance. Now the vice president of marketing for Baxa Corporation, Marian has more than 25 years experience in medical device manufacturing and marketing communications. She has been an active member of the Colorado chapter of the Business Marketing Association since 2005. Marian holds a master's degree in policy and planning from The University of Michigan.

# 11 | Telling Your Company Story From the Inside Out

Carla Johnson

As a kid, I hated history. It was boring. It didn't matter. And I didn't care. But a funny thing happened on the way to graduation. One of my high-school teachers changed my perception of history and inspired me to learn more in one year than in the previous ten combined.

Sometimes, our perceptions about the companies for which we work may feel the same way. We show up. They pay us. Together we figure out answers. We all move from one year to the next.

We've learned that corporate rebranding and external campaigns often generate the lion's share of work we do as marketers.

> *"Companies of all sizes have an opportunity to refresh and ingrain their brands while building employee engagement using an oft-overlooked tool — their corporate history."*

They're sexy. They have budget. And, they get attention. As B2B marketers, these provide benchmarks to justify budgets and headcount. They keep our brand in front of the market and rally employees. Logos, taglines and campaign themes all push messages of what a company delivers and how it outranks the competition.

But rarely do marketing and history mix. This chapter, however, puts history back into the equation. Companies of all sizes have an opportunity to refresh and ingrain their brands while building employee engagement using an oft-overlooked tool — their corporate history.

## Why We're Here

People start companies for a reason. But over the years, the bigger picture of why we're here often gets lost in the frenzy of daily priorities, quarterly projections and annual revenue. As years pass, employees may lack focus and customers may lose their emotional connection to a company without a common thread holding everyone together. That common thread is history.

When a company goes back to the basics and tells the story of why it's here, employees make an emotional connection. When employees are engaged, it helps them represent the company's brand. And when employees understand how their piece of the puzzle affects the overall performance of a company, they go out of their way to create better customer experiences.

## Putting the STORY Into Corporate History

Some companies develop their corporate history as a timeline with a couple of sentences describing major milestones. But this doesn't tell the story of why, where and how it began; the challenges and celebrations along the way; and how the company influenced, or was impacted by, the world around them. Timelines share facts, not connections.

Creating a corporate history that people — employees, alumni, investors, stockholders, media, influencers and so forth — want to read shouldn't involve an academic approach. It doesn't have to take years to produce. It doesn't require a Ph.D. in history. It simply needs to tell the story.

### The Steps

Sitting down to plan your corporate history project might feel like a tremendous challenge. It's one thing to get your arms around the project; it's another to know what it is you need to get your arms around. The following guidelines may help you get started.

**Step 1. Determine who should be involved and their responsibilities. Consider including:**
- **Project Sponsor** — Someone in marketing or communications who has ultimate responsibility for the quality and delivery of the project. This person will need the authority to secure a budget for the project, and gain input and support from the management team and appropriate employees.
- **Project Manager** — This person holds responsibility for the day-to-day interactions and ensures that the project stays on schedule. He or she serves as the point person for any outside support, such as writing, design and printing.

- **Historian/Corporate Archivist/Corporate Librarian** — If you have someone who maintains historical records and materials, their input will help the team know what resources are readily available.
- **Legal** – Because the information included in a corporate history will be repurposed, it's important to have a legal team review all content to ensure that it meets the appropriate guidelines and requirements.
- **Writer/Researcher** — Ideally, one person will perform both these functions, which ultimately streamlines the process. The best fit is someone who understands marketing, branding and historical writing.
- **Graphic Designer** — A designer with a strong background as an art director can help with creative concepts. The right designer will also have experience working with printing firms, and can share options about printing and binding during your early conversations.
- **Photographer** — Some companies have a photographer on staff or have a regular one with whom they work. If not, most writers and graphics designers have contacts.

### Step 2. Take inventory of the available materials
- Annual reports
- Marketing/advertising campaigns
- Maps, graphs, any other images
- Outside articles written about the company and published online, in newspapers, magazines, etc.
- Photos from company events

### Step 3. Fill gaps through research. Supplement your inventory with additional information.
- Telephone or in-person interviews
  - Current employees, such as the executive team; long-term employees who have experienced change; employees in other parts of the world
  - Vendors who have watched and helped the company grow over time
  - Former employees, including executives who made decisions about the direction of the company
  - Industry analysts
- Museum artifacts, historical society accounts and other public organization archives

- Events that took place during the life of the company and how they may have impacted, or been impacted by, the company

## Step 4. Determine budget

- **Research/Writing** — Your writer will need to account for the amount of time he or she will need for research, and how difficult some of the research may be to conduct. Are interviewees in different parts of the country or world? Are they available via phone, or will e-mail provide sufficient information? If your legal team prefers to receive source or other documentation for all material, this may double and even triple the amount of time normally dedicated to this type of research and writing project.
- **Graphic Design** — What size book would you like to produce? Is it a soft-cover that's saddle stitched in the middle? Or is it an oversize piece with a hard cover and stitched at the binding? Do you prefer four-color images or will black and white do? How many "comps" (samples of different layouts from which to choose) do you prefer to review? Will your designer be involved in reviewing proofs during the printing process?
- **Photography** — Will you need new photography? If so, in how many locations will your photographer need to shoot? Can everything be done in a day? Will you need to hire multiple photographers in multiple locations? Will you need product images or updated pictures of company executives?
- **Printing** — How many copies? What kind of paper? If your company focuses heavily on sustainability, the paper, ink and cover selections you make may impact your budget. Also, do you need the printer to ship copies nationally or internationally?
- **Photo Rights** — Will you need to pay photographers, public figures or other companies for the rights to use their images or logos?

## Step 5. Develop and produce the content

- You may have an idea of how you want the book structured, or you may ask your writer to provide an outline. There's no set rule on how to organize your corporate history as long as the story flows smoothly and it all makes sense. For some companies, organizing chronologically proves best. For others, describing major areas of their business and how they fit into the big picture makes more sense. Regardless, it's best to organize the structure at the beginning and have the team agree in order to save time (and money) down the road.

- Ideally, your writer and designer will work together to coordinate what images support the text, and what images can stand alone yet still help tell the story.

- From here, the development and production process follows the same approach as any marketing piece. Have the content reviewers approve the copy and the images with captions and then drop them into the layout. Review, revise and repeat. Just like similar projects, you'll need a strong dose of patience to keep everyone focused on the main goal of the project during the review cycle.

- Once you have content approval and legal has secured all the necessary rights, you or your designer will work with the printer on production, including approvals, quantity, due dates and shipping, if needed.

## CASE STUDY
## Western Union — A New Company With a 160-Year History

**The Client and the Challenge.** During its history, Western Union received credit for its many outstanding, history-making achievements. In 2006, the company celebrated its 155th year in business and also prepared for its split from First Data Corporation, which acquired the company in 1995. A newly independent company, Western Union sought to educate employees, businesses, agents and consumers on the significant contributions that the company made from the inception of the electric telegraph in 1844 through the day in 2006 when it again became an independently owned and operated company.

Few people, including long-time employees, realized the role Western Union played in modern history. The strategy behind the company's corporate history was to "tell the tale" of the company with an easy-to-read, oversized "coffee-table" style book rich with historic telegrams, photographs, maps, postcards and advertising images. *The Western Union Story* sought to share the chronological story of the company's focus on serving businesses and consumers.

**The Journey.** During the development of the project, the team agreed the best way to tell the company's story was to use a chronological format, with special sections inserted between chapters that focused on areas of particular interest. The timeline transitioned into the book's table of contents.

Introduction

Chapter 1 – 1791-1840s: Giving the World a Voice
· The Founders of Western Union

Chapter 2 – 1850s-1860s: Early Days of Western Union
· Transcontinental Telegraph

Chapter 3 – 1860s-1870s: Becoming a Global Leader
· Money Transfer

Chapter 4 – 1870s-1900s: Connecting People and Businesses
· Time Ball/Time Service

Chapter 5 – 1910s-1930s: Golden Age of Messengers and Telegrams
· Famous Telegrams
· Messengers

Chapter 6 – 1940s: The World at War
· Hollywood

Chapter 7 – 1950s-1960s: Business Boom
· Specialty Telegrams

Chapter 8 – 1970s-1980s: New Communications Frontiers
· Advertising/Telegram Art

Chapter 9 – 1990s-2000s: Redefining Western Union
· Global Reach

Chapter 10 – Our History: Prologue for the Future
· From Disaster Relief to the Western Union Foundation
· NYSE Bell Ringing

**The Implementation.** Western Union has an excellent inventory of visual and graphic elements that helped illustrate its historical achievements. Images proved key to bringing the company's history to life: the completion of the first transcontinental telegraph line; involvement in the U.S. purchase of the Alaska territory from Russia; famous telegrams (the Wright brothers from Kitty Hawk, the Zimmerman Telegram); famous employees (Patti Page, Will Rogers); and, the launch of the first U.S. domestic communications satellite into space.

Western Union values its rich heritage, which is supported by the company's investment in an archivist. This person's responsibility is to maintain the company's existing historical documents and secure others available publically or through donations from former employees. The challenge in maintaining a thorough collection of corporate records, annual reports, communications, advertising and other historical documents comes from the company changing ownership throughout its history. Unfortunately, some holding companies did not see the long-term value in preserving and protecting documents and disposed of them along the way.

Because the book serves as the corporate history for Western Union, the company took every step to ensure that the details were historically correct. Throughout the research and writing process, all original sources for information were provided to the Western Union legal and intellectual property team as supporting evidence of the accuracy of the information. In addition, the legal team secured any rights needed to include images of celebrities, scenes from movies, company employees and third-party publications that included Western Union advertising.

**The Results.** In a mere six months, Western Union moved the corporate history from an idea and an outline to a beautiful, leather-bound book rich with stories and images of the company's 150-year history. Within a month of Western Union becoming independently owned and operated, the company distributed copies of *The Western Union Story* to employees around the world. The book has helped employees connect with Western Union and understand its legacy in communications and the different ways in which the company still connects people across the globe. It has proven a common tie for a broadly scattered global workforce.

Today, new employees still receive a copy when they join the company. The head of employee communications (formerly the archivist on this project) often receives calls or e-mails from employees asking for "a copy of the photo on page XX." Many people have framed photos from the book hanging in their offices. Some have even been used in presentations. In addition, the company president and other executives frequently give copies as gifts to government officials and other key influencers.

## Summary

From telegraphs and telefaxes to worldwide money transfer, Western Union took advantage of its corporate history to unite a growing global employee base and to remind businesses and consumers of how the company helps people everywhere stay connected.

For many of us, history class is a memory. But all companies have a wonderful opportunity to draw on the stories from their corporate history to engage employees and refresh and rejuvenate their brand throughout the marketplace.

---

Western Union succumbed to Chapter 11 bankruptcy in 1993 and was purchased in a 1994 bankruptcy court auction by First Financial Management Corporation (FFMC). The following year, FFMC merged with First Data Corporation, and Western Union became a subsidiary.

 **Carla Johnson** is president of Type A Communications and 2010-2011 president of BMA Colorado. With a career in marketing, PR and employee communications and a master's degree in history, she helps companies draw on their history to develop their purpose and strengthen their brands internally with employees and externally with clients, prospects and investors. In addition to *The Western Union Story*, Carla has managed and written *Projects, Products and Services: Celebrating 75 Years of Excellence* for the U.S. Army Corps of Engineers, Omaha District, and *Union Pacific and Omaha Union Station*, currently in its 4th printing. Her work has received numerous awards from BMA, PRSA, IABC and industry-specific organizations. Carla has been a member of BMA Colorado since 2007.

# 12 | Ten Steps to Integrating Social Media

Tom Schippert

Corporate communications is not always thought of as a media play, but that's what the Internet has effectively done for B2B communications. The biggest issue facing these businesses is still a classic public relations and communications quandary: What does the company do? What's interesting about it? And how is an effective online plan built that gets the brand and company noticed in the media?

> *"Internet marketing programs, like all other marketing initiatives, are designed with specific goals in mind."*

The best marketing programs are developed through planning, strategic design and budgeting. Internet marketing programs are no different. From e-mail marketing to search engine optimization (SEO) to website design and blogging, there are literally dozens of ways a marketing budget can be eviscerated with these strategies. Add social media tactics and you have to spend even more time and money creating a relevant brand. These are the challenges businesses face week-in, week-out, and month-in, month-out.

Companies can be overwhelmed making the jump to the Internet or invigorating their online presence. To make things easier, here are ten steps businesses can take to build a compelling Internet Marketing program.

**Step 1. Understand corporate needs and culture.** Corporate culture can be a driver of Internet strategy, or not. For example, a client business was wary of creating a website, thinking it might be detrimental to its business model and the nature of how it interacts with customers. But, embracing this culture led to effectively guiding management through the integration of their website with social media and growing the business as opposed to hurting it. By making the case that creating this change in corporate culture would lead to stronger growth, management began to understand the power of the Internet in transforming the culture and the company.

**Step 2. Establish goals.** Internet marketing programs, like all other marketing initiatives, are designed with specific goals in mind. Should a company include a blog to effectively inform audiences about positions that affect the business? Will a searchable catalog of products and services lead to sales? Would a promotional site centered on a specific sweepstakes or incentive increase the brand's prominence? Should the company focus on its image and provide a site that highlights the brand promise and position? These are all worthwhile goals, but the trick is to develop and define goals that make sense in relation to the company's products, services, time commitment and budget.

**Step 3. Determine roles and responsibilities.** Scheduling time and resources to consistently execute online marketing programs can be a challenge. Dedicating manpower and giving individuals distinct duties can lead to an ongoing online presence. But be selective, because each activity takes time and some choices are more effective than others. The goal is to select those tactics that work best for your business and extend the brand ubiquitously.

**Step 4. Plan content.** Content development and distribution is the cornerstone of online creativity. A solid content plan is integral to building a strong case with audiences and sharing valuable information about your business. This includes identifying storylines and comments and how they'll appear online — whether as a blog post, social media entry, online video or audio podcast. Developing an editorial calendar helps outline the narrative from which entries can be developed and be shared across the most effective social media platforms available.

**Step 5. Conduct research and share insights.** A key benefit of online marketing is sharing research and insights that are interesting to core audiences. By highlighting key facts and case studies that provide value to potential clients, a business can build brand equity as well-informed experts. Links to other sites and Web resources elevate the host site's prominence, delivering stronger search results and wider exposure for the business. There is a caveat, however. When sharing information online, cite sources and authors and be transparent about the nature of the data and information.

**Step 6. Choose social media and delivery platforms.** Companies must adapt to today's technologies by choosing those that are best for their business. For example, if a company has a presence on LinkedIn, does it also need a business page on Facebook? Should a company build a blog site from scratch, or would leveraging a website that achieves the same goal be a better choice? What key industry and association sites are available to the company, and how can they benefit the organization? Would incorporating Twitter drive audiences to the site, or do these target groups rarely access Twitter? What industry-related social media sites can be leveraged? When considering renewed site design, does an HTML site make sense, or would a WordPress-based site that maximizes interactivity be a better choice? These are just a few of the questions a business needs to ask because today's Internet is like the Wild West. Choices are abundant and each activity costs a business time, effort and money. Therefore, it's extremely important to define top choices and understand how they will benefit the organization.

**Step 7. Develop processes and training.** Every online technology and website has its own protocols and functionality. A business must dedicate resources and time for training to use them to their top potential. For example, Twitter and WordPress take development training to use properly. Clients learn about the various methods of posting and sharing on Twitter, what the various signs and keys are and what they do. Businesses are also shown tools such as HootSuite that manage online assets efficiently. WordPress clients learn about widgets and plug-ins that can be incorporated to help create a truly interactive experience for site visitors. Building a flawless user experience requires training on how to utilize Web and social media programs. It's something all businesses must consider as they look to get the most out of their online strategies.

**Step 8. Be committed to an ongoing campaign.** Traditional marketing programs are effective because they are designed to influence audiences over an extended period of time. The same is true online. There must be a dedicated, ongoing commitment to reaching out on a consistent basis. Building a solid content plan is one component; having defined roles and responsibilities is another. But most importantly, the commitment must come from the company's leadership to ensure that the company's brand is continuously present online. It means being committed to online marketing and developing the resources that will consistently share the brand's position and value with online audiences.

**Step 9. Track site usage and analytics.** Usage patterns that lead audiences to Web and social media sites change rapidly. Current headlines, items that are posted on the site and interactive elements all lead to audience interaction with the brand. To capture these trends, it's important to build tracking and analytical tools that reveal traffic patterns and reflect how individuals access the site. Tools like Google Analytics offer a full range of features, including lists, tables and charts. The WordPress website and blog platform has analytical tools built-in, and many e-mail management tools, like Constant Contact and others, include data components related to e-mail campaign performance. Monthly, and sometimes weekly, analysis lets a business quickly identify functionality that works best on the site and make adjustments.

**Step 10. Adjust and change direction as needed.** Marketing is an ever-changing and evolving process. Although the goal is to create a plan that a company can follow closely, businesses must be flexible so that they can change direction and make creative adjustments based on analytical results of their campaigns and customer feedback. The marketer should be prepared to change the plan, add new elements, remove some, and follow patterns revealed by the site's analytics.

## CASE STUDY
## The Villager Newspaper

**The Challenge.** The Villager Newspaper in Greenwood Village, Colorado, had all intentions of creating an online presence. However, with valuable subscribers and advertisers committed to the weekly printed newspaper, the publisher worried that an online version might overshadow the print newspaper and limit the impact of paid advertising. Although a thriving newspaper with a strong and loyal subscription base can be a rarity in today's media climate, the publisher decided to seize the promise of "new media" and embrace reaching out to audiences through Internet technologies.

**The Journey.** The journey began by creating a need and convincing the publisher about the value of extending The Villager Newspaper brand online. Client buy-in is always a key component of success in marketing, and this marketing program would only be successful if management could motivate staff to enact new activities and direction. In addition, it's the marketer's job to gauge a project's budget and prepare business owners for the commitment required for success. The key for The Villager was to create a versatile site on the WordPress platform that would provide full interactivity and thrust the business into the Internet age.

**The Discovery.** Although the company's management was wary about placing an edition online, they knew that it would help solidify the brand with subscribers and the community. Even so, they had to be nudged to make it happen by the hired consulting group. Upon deeper discussion, the project was outlined and broken down as a series of ten steps. Through this process the online objectives became more understandable and palatable to the business owners. And, the guidance provided became endearing to management, creating trust with the consulting team.

This trust-building transformed into excitement on the part of the company's owners. Presenting a succinct plan to the company's management, and clearly explaining the value of new technologies in online and website development, led to greater understanding. Plus, sharing long-term expertise in agency- and communications-planning activities forged a strong relationship with management and they discovered that taking their business into the Internet age could be accomplished through planning and trust.

**The Solution.** By working closely together through the ten-step process and identifying the online strategy, key steps were established that would give the publisher tools to bring readers unique insights in an ongoing fashion. An integral part of the strategy was to utilize the WordPress platform to build a fully interactive, dynamic website. It also increased SEO performance, as the interactive nature of the pages and the use of backlinks improved search performance. And, of course, the paper's fresh and relevant reporting and content also helped the site get found online.

In addition to the new website, the company needed a way to tease online audiences to visit the site's pages, draw-in new readers and raise interest in the printed edition. Twitter and Facebook pages bring in audiences, and scheduled daily "tweets" highlight featured articles.

These technical solutions are cornerstones for extending the company's brand and bringing its range of topics and reporting to a wider audience through integrated websites and social media properties.

**The Implementation.** The website's design and set-up was implemented through closely followed organized steps and deadlines. After training the staff on how to manipulate the program, create news posts, add images and reply to comments, this new site helped The Villager access a wider audience than they ever had before. Popular columns and compelling writing also brought audiences to the site. As a trusted news source in Denver for many years, the publishers sought new ways to present its perspectives and columnists in the city's news environment. In fact, Chuck Green, a longtime popular Denver editorialist, received more than 400 comments and evoked lively discussion through one of his columns.

To really maximize the effects of Twitter online, an editorial calendar was developed that scheduled tweets to highlight stories or breaking news. This gave the paper a strategic edge in continuously promoting its news by releasing "teasers" on a scheduled basis throughout the day. To make the Twitter component even more ubiquitous, training was held in regard to Twitter's codes and message distribution methods. It helped the editor determine which stories to highlight through Twitter for the paper's readers and still follow the editorial calendar's guidelines.

The company's page on Facebook helped extend the online brand and create even more viral activity as users shared content and informed "friends" that they "like" the site, inviting them to visit the pages as well. By addressing any technical hurdles and adhering to a strategic approach of posting content, the publisher successfully launched the site, and extended the brand to a wide and engaged online audience.

**The Results.** Not only was an interactive website developed through the versatile WordPress platform, it integrated social media assets that would play an important part in drawing new readers to the paper's fresh reporting and community stories. One outcome was that management came to fully endorse the use of WordPress for the website. Owners also found value in adding social media sites and other interactive tactics that would keep readers on, and engaged with, the site.

When the online edition broke an important story and beat the large local news sources to the scoop, it gave the paper an edge on local reporting, immediacy and relevance to online and offline readers. Readers were informed of the situation through Twitter and Facebook and quickly accessed the website to learn about details.

The scenario was a measurable success in reporting and delivering relevant news to readers quickly. It also increased the perceived value of the paper in the community. Now, readers can follow local news and developments by following tweets, and access breaking news instantly online rather than learning of news items in the weekly print version.

In fact, the site has received thousands of visits since it was first introduced, and visitations have increased as readers share the site's news through integrated Web and social media. (See chart for monthly and total visits to the site.)

Not only are visits being driven through Twitter, readers are also driven to the site by The Villager's Facebook page where 'friends' can access links to stories directly through the website. Search optimization practices also drive visitors through Google, Facebook, Wikipedia, Google Maps, Yahoo and AOL.

| The Villager Newspaper 2010 Monthly Website Visits | |
|---|---|
| April | 5,147 |
| May | 6,476 |
| June | 6,543 |
| July | 6,104 |
| Aug. | 8,057 |
| Sept. | 7,960 |
| April — Sept. Total Visits | 44,480 |

Blog aggregator sites, like Mondo Times and Feedburner, also bring traffic to the Web pages. There's also access through RSS feeds such as Google Reader, giving readers the flexibility to receive their news on topics that interest them most. And, local government and education sites that feature a story from the paper drive traffic back to the site.

Another key element is identifying keywords that visitors enter to find the site and its news. What's interesting, and useful, is to understand the many ways the company's brand is remembered and searched for online. For example, here is a sample list of search terms that users entered when looking for information, or the source itself. Notice the numerous permutations of "The Villager." Even if details about the newspaper were inaccurate in their mind, searchers remembered the brand name and found the site by entering any of a number of different terms.

Content-wise, the company doesn't post every story that appears in the print version. This lets the print paper retain its value with audiences and ensures that advertisements influence readers. But the online version of the paper complements the print version and has proven to be a smart business decision. Accord-

| The Villager Newspaper Sample Search Terms |
|---|
| arapahoe county media |
| bob sweeney, greenwood villager |
| cherry hills village newspaper |
| greenwood village colorado newspaper |
| southwest denver herald dispatch |
| the greenwood villager |
| the villager Colorado |
| the villager Denver |
| the villager greenwood village |
| the villager newspaper littleton, co |
| the villager paper |
| the villager publishing company |
| the villager, chuck green |
| thevillager centennial |
| villager publications greenwood village |
| villager publishing denver tech center |
| www.villagerpublishing.com |

ing to Saundra Sweeney: "Taking the paper online was a big step for us in both strategy and resources. We knew we'd have to use all the social media and interactive features available in this crowded media environment. It's made a big difference in spreading our news to more readers on a daily basis, and it bolsters our weekly paper. We're now really delivering what our readers look for from us, and we're becoming even more of an important part of the community than we have ever been before."

## Taking the Ten Steps to Success

Newspapers are working to develop the same impact for readers online that they have traditionally provided through the printed word. Media companies have come a long way in a short time by pioneering some of the most interactive elements on the Internet. By taking the ten steps outlined here, businesses of all types can transform their business and successfully integrate Web and social media properties to their utmost benefit.

**Tom Schippert**, principal of Tom Schippert Communications, provides specialized experience in strategic communications planning, Internet marketing, public relations and copywriting. His professional background combines years of public relations agency and corporate communications experience that allows him to bring creative insights to various marketing endeavors. Schippert holds a master's degree in communications management from Colorado State University and a bachelor's degree in mass communications and journalism from the University of Denver. Tom joined BMA Colorado in 2008 and, in 2010, was its CareerLink Chairperson.

# 13 Just Give Me the Facts
## Literalism vs. Symbolism in B2B Advertising

Maria van Dessel, Ph.D. and Charles H. Patti, Ph.D.

For decades the prevailing idea in B2B marketing has been that buyers are motivated by product/service specifications. Sellers are put on approved supplier lists, invited to respond to request for proposals (RFP), and are selected on the basis of superior products, at the right price, delivered on time. The history of B2B advertising is filled with the advice "provide product specifications" and your advertising will be noticed, lead to sales inquiries, and eventually result in higher sales. Advertising filled with abstractions might work in the B2C market, but the B2B marketplace is about being literal.

What we know about advertising — and particularly the message component of advertising — is based on a combination of experience, unproven ideas and a bit of social science. Over the years, advertising guidelines produced by the predecessors of BMA (National Industrial Advertising Association, Association of Industrial Advertising, and the Business/Professional Advertising Association) stressed emphasizing product features and tangible benefits. The major publishers of B2B magazines, e.g., McGraw-Hill, Penton Publishing, et al. had similar recommendations. Also, B2B marketing books recommend advertising that focuses on specific product features (Kotler and Pfoertsch, 2006; Lamons, 2005).

In more recent times, abstraction in advertising messages has penetrated the B2B marketplace. Even though such advertising legends as David Ogilvy (1963, 1985) frequently recommended advertising based on hard-core information, there has been the growing use of emotional appeals, including humor, fear, parental affection, etc. Beyond the use of emotion, marketers attempt to build a stronger connection between their brands and buyers through the use of abstraction and symbolism. Below are two examples of B2B advertisements — Figure 1A is high in literalism and Figure 1B is high in symbolism. Which approach — a "left-brain" (literal) or "right brain" (symbolic) is more effective in B2B advertising? Are the advertising message-creation guidelines from the history of B2B advertising accurate? Are the foundations of B2B message creation (experience and unproven ideas) sound?

## Protelco Corporation: Who's Right?

Protelco was founded by Tom and Edward Dittmer in 2002. The company is a leading supplier of software voice platforms to hosting service companies, telecommunications carriers, and other large businesses that require touch-tone and speech recognition solutions. Its software platforms help clients provide a superior experience for the clients' customers through improved caller satisfaction. The rapid growth of call centers — along with the products developed by Tom and Ed and their R&D staff — has created a profitable and steadily growing company in Protelco.

Figure 1A: Highly Literal B2B Advertisement

The growth of the industry has drawn many other companies into the marketplace, and today, Protelco faces a highly competitive environment with dozens of small and large companies competing on product superiority, price and service. The service component includes problem-solving abilities, installation and training expertise, and after-sale service.

Figure 1B: Highly Symbolic B2B Advertisement

While Protelco offers several different products and services, Tom and Ed recently decided to focus their attention on the marketing of their interactive voice response (IVR) product. IVR software is widely used because it allows a computer to detect voice and keypad inputs. The result is that callers can get instructions and solve their own problems or get answers to their questions by following instructions without a live interface. In turn, this creates significant efficiencies for the company and, in most cases, a better experience for the caller. In some ways, this technology can be compared to the now-omnipresent ATM machine or airline check-in kiosks — systems that at first were perceived as a lesser service, but over time, users find more convenient and efficient than a personal interaction with a company representative.

IVR software is used extensively in the telecommunications industry, online retailing (when calling is used), and more recently in the automobile industry for hands-free operation of navigation, entertainment, and mobile phone systems. In order to reach buyers of IVR systems, Tom and Ed decided to supplement their Web-based marketing programs with print advertisements in the trade magazines that reach potential buyers. The purpose of their new advertising campaign is to introduce Protelco to potential buyers, explain the advantages of Protelco's IVR software, to position the company as a first-class problem solver, and to generate leads for their personal sales representatives. To execute the new campaign, Tom and Ed hired a local communications agency that was known for its skill in B2B marketing thinking and developing comprehensive marketing communications programs. In preparation for the first meeting with the agency's representatives, Tom and Ed requested that their marketing research department examine the marketplace to see what information would be helpful in the development of the marketing communications campaign.

## Market Research Information

For two months before the first meeting, the Protelco marketing research department undertook a study of the marketplace to help understand buying patterns and behavior. The study included a sample of the company's current IVR customers and a sample of prospective customers. A questionnaire was developed and e-mailed to this sample. After a four-week period, which included two reminder e-mails to encourage response, 251 usable questionnaires were received. After analyzing the responses, the following tables were presented to Tom, Ed, and the agency's representatives.

Table 1: Motives for Purchasing IVR Software

| Motives for purchasing IVR software | Importance score (1= low importance; 5= high importance) | |
| --- | --- | --- |
| | Current customers | Prospective customers |
| Dissatisfaction with current vendor | 4.0 | 1.1 |
| Need to increase operating efficiency | 4.0 | 4.2 |
| Desire to enhance customer experience | 4.3 | 3.8 |
| Development of new products in our product mix | 2.3 | 2.0 |

**Table 2: Reasons for Selection of Particular Vendor**

| Reasons for brand/company vendor selection | Importance rank (1= most important) | |
| --- | --- | --- |
| | Current customers | Prospective customers |
| State of the art software | 5 | 4 |
| Problem-solving ability | 4 | 3 |
| Price and financial terms | 7 | 5 |
| Installation service | 6 | 7 |
| Ongoing service | 3 | 6 |
| Industry reputation, including testimonials | 2 | 1 |
| Stability of vendor | 1 | 2 |

# Development of Advertising Message Strategy

**The first meeting.** Tom and Edward Dittmer were very concerned about the overall impression of the new advertising campaign. During their first meeting, the agency account supervisor, Bill Mayes, outlined ideas for the advertising campaign. He suggested that the message should stress Protelco's reputation in the industry and their stability — even though they haven't been in business as long as some of the other competitors. Bill also wanted to weave in the idea of prospects being dissatisfied with their current vendor. Bill's rationale for this approach was based primarily on the data in Tables 1 and 2 (for both current and prospective customers). On the other hand, the Dittmers had a completely different idea. They felt that they had built their business on the basis of helping customers improve their operating efficiency and by providing excellent installation and ongoing service. These attributes also scored well in the customer and prospect survey. Furthermore, they felt that Bill's ideas would be too "soft" for the marketplace, not hitting hard enough on factual information that Protelco could provide. At the end of the meeting, Bill left to develop more specific advertising strategy ideas.

**The second meeting and more challenges.** When Bill returned and made a more formal presentation to Tom and Edward, he presented two alternative strategies.

### Strategy A. The Dittmers' approach: Traditional B2B advertising

*"Buy Protelco's IVR system because it has been proven to increase customers' operating efficiency by 15 percent and depending on the size of the company, that*

*translates into millions of dollars saved each year. A secondary reason to buy is Protelco's award-winning installation and ongoing service."*

The print ads, the website, and all other marketing communication materials would focus on the facts that support the two main reasons to buy from Protelco. Visuals would show money being saved from improved operating efficiency, installation staff working closely with customers on initial installation as well as follow up service.

### Strategy B. The Bill Mayes approach: High-quality image

*"Buy Protelco's IVR system because the company's stability and reputation will overcome prospective customers' dissatisfaction with current vendors."*

The print ads, the website, and all other marketing communication materials would focus on a series of images that communicate stability, reputation and dissatisfaction. For example, Bill already has the agency's art department working on symbols of these attributes, including images of Stonehenge (stability), Galapagos turtles (stability), athletic teams losing a match at the last second (disappointment), Abraham Lincoln and George Washington (reputation), etc. The idea was to attract the attention of the reader through these striking and interesting visuals and then link them through copy to the stability and reputation of Protelco — and how doing business with Protelco would eliminate dissatisfaction of working with other vendors.

At the end of the second meeting, nobody could agree on what to do. Both strategies had potential, but they were very different from each other. The Dittmers argued that the traditional wisdom about how to generate high readership among B2B buyers was grounded in literal advertising messages — facts about the product/service and the specific, material benefits that would follow from the advertising product/service attributes. The brothers weren't much interested in risking their company's money on an advertising campaign that seemed to be much removed from the traditions of B2B advertising.

Bill argued that a changing media environment and more sophisticated buyers meant that it was impossible to get B2B ads noticed and read without interesting visuals and copy that would stretch the imagination of readers. Bill also pointed to the trends toward the use of symbolism in B2C advertising, saying that this trend is likely to find its way into the B2B sector.

**Moving Forward.** When agreement could not be reached, Bill suggested that his agency undertake a research project to see which type of

B2B advertisements (literal or symbolic) are more effective at producing higher readership scores. The Dittmer brothers agreed and the research staff at Bill's agency initiated the study, getting relevant materials from GfK Starch Communications, and organizing a content analysis of over 500 B2B print advertisements.

**The Study.** The purpose of the study was to determine the comparative effectiveness of literalism and symbolism in generating Starch readership scores. To conduct the study, three coders were trained to look for literal and symbolic content and to code the sample advertisements. The advertisements shown are examples high in literalism (Figure 1A) and high in symbolism (Figure 1B) (see p. 112). At the end of two weeks, 508 full-page, color B2B print advertisements were coded and their scores on literalism and symbolism were compared to the ads' Starch scores. Literalism-symbolism was scored on a seven-point scale, where 1=highly literal and 7=highly symbolic. The scores from the study are shown in Tables 3 and 4.

**Table 3: Literalism-Symbolism Across Three Industries**

| Industry Examined | Number of ads coded | Literalism-Symbolism Score (1=highly literal; 7=highly symbolic) |
|---|---|---|
| A (architecture) | 182 | 4.1 |
| B (software) | 201 | 3.6 |
| C (aviation) | 125 | 3.7 |
| Totals | 508 | 3.8 |

**Post-study meeting and the study results.** First, it was surprising to everyone that the overall score on literalism-symbolism was only 3.8 — slightly above the mid-point on the seven-point scale. However, the highest "literalism" score was among advertisements in the software industry. The Dittmers took this as support for their position for traditional advertising message strategy. Second, three

> *"Based on the study results, literal advertisements are no more effective than symbolic ads in generating readership scores."*

factors were examined against the four levels of Starch readership. The literalism-symbolism factor was not significant in terms of explaining any level of Starch readership.

Table 4: Factors Affecting Starch Readership Scores

| Factor | Levels of Starch Readership | | | |
| --- | --- | --- | --- | --- |
| | Noted | Associated | Read Some | Read Most |
| Literalism-Symbolism | Not Significant | Not Significant | Not Significant | Not Significant |
| Industry (three industries examined) | 4% | 3% | 6% | 10% |
| Mechanical variables (length of headline, amount of body copy, size of visual) | 8% | 6% | 3% | Not Significant |

**Challenges to traditional B2B thinking.** Should Protelco's new advertising campaign take a literal or symbolic approach? Based on the study results, literal advertisements are no more effective than symbolic ads in generating readership scores. Could this be true? After all, decades of B2B advertisement wisdom tell us that B2B buyers want, need, and respond to literal, factual, rational messages. Even Bill was surprised by the results of the study. He had no scientific support for his recommendations using a symbolic approach. But, neither did the Dittmers. The Dittmers' recommendation of message strategy was based on their understanding of B2B traditions.

**In the end, the Dittmers accepted Bill's recommendation.** The agency implemented a campaign largely based on the ideas expressed in Strategy B. Starch readership measures were taken on the Protelco campaign at the six- and twelve-month periods and the scores were slightly above industry averages. Protelco successfully fought off the increased competition and while their market share growth rate slowed, they continued to grow and they remain a powerful force in the IVR software market.

## Lessons Learned From the Protelco Case

There is much to be learned from a close examination of the practices of any company. Good practices can almost always be extended successfully across industry sectors just as they can across countries. The more we notice, the more we know. The Protelco case gives us at least three good lessons.

1. **Beware of so-called, time-tested principles.** Assumptions are dangerous in any field — and perhaps none more than in marketing where so little is proven. Ideas that might have worked well in one era are passed on with the assumption that they will work in all environ-

ments. This is rarely effective. The Protelco case is a good example of how assumptions from the past can be seriously flawed today yet continue to invade our thinking. The idea of "just give me the facts" apparently is not as true as many think. Holding on to traditional and often unproven ideas about advertising can be a dangerous approach to developing effective advertising.

2. **Invest in research before launching into major marketing initiatives.** To their credit, Protelco and Mayes's agency took the time and effort to design and execute a study to help guide their decision. And, while at some level, the study's results were not completely conclusive, they did show that literalism is no more effective than symbolism in generating readership scores in the B2B marketplace. This result will have a lasting effect on Bill Mayes and the Dittmers as they plan future marketing communications programs. They learned to question their own assumptions and other, unproven traditions.

3. **Walk before you leap onto the next big idea.** There is no shortage of new ideas about marketing, including marketing communication. Few of them have staying power and many are not grounded in anything more than superficial observations. Learning how to balance being open to new ideas with being critical is not simple. While it's true that "every path has its puddle," if we never go down the path, we'll never get to the next place. Even though Bill's idea of using a symbolism-based campaign was not a completely new idea, it broke from traditions in B2B advertising — and it was a significant departure from Protelco's history of using more literal marketing communications messages. To the Dittmers' credit, they were open to considering Bill's approach, but they were cautious enough to push for more research.

Kotler, Philip, and Waldemar Pfoertsch. *B2B Brand Management*. Berlin-Heidelberg, Germany: Springer, 2006.

Lamons, Bob. *The Case for B2B Branding*. Mason, Ohio: Thomson-Southwestern, 2005.

Ogilvy, David. *Confessions of an Advertising Man*. New York: Atheneum, 1963.

Ogilvy, David. *Ogilvy on Advertising*. New York: Knopf Doubleday Publishing, 1985.

**Maria van Dessel** holds a Ph.D. degree from Queensland University of Technology, Brisbane, Australia where she is also a tenured faculty member in the School of Advertising, Marketing and Public Relations. Her research focuses on the general area of marketing communication and her doctoral dissertation investigated advertising message types in B2B advertising, seeking to evaluate the effect of symbolic and literal messages on advertising performance. Maria has presented her research at international conferences — in Australia, the Czech Republic, and the United States. She teaches courses in advertising, marketing, and ethics in marketing communications.

**Charles H. Patti** is the James M. Cox Professor of Customer Experience Management at the University of Denver. He has a long career in B2B marketing and higher education — as a faculty member, senior executive, consultant, and author of dozens of articles and cases, books, and industry reports. Professor Patti has extensive international experience, including visiting professorships in Finland, Italy, England, New Zealand, Singapore, and Malaysia. Prior to rejoining the University of Denver in 2006, he was the Head of the School of Advertising, Marketing, and Public Relations at Queensland University of Technology, Brisbane, Australia. In addition to this academic position, Dr. Patti has an active profile in industry through consulting, boards, collaborations, and expert witness assignments. Dr. Patti was a long-time BMA Colorado member in the 1980s and rejoined in 2008.

# IMPLEMENTING YOUR PLAN

ADVICE FROM THE TOP

# 14 | Improving Partner Relationships in Today's Competitive Landscape

Scott Gillum

I n nearly every industry, business partners play an important role in a company's distribution and go-to-market strategy, but the relationship between vendors and partners has not always been a smooth one. Often times, partners are hailed as important channels to key customers on one day, and then condemned as needy, never satisfied and disloyal the next. And partners themselves often have conflicted perspectives that may be fueled by confusion and frustration from inconsistent in-channel marketing programs, sales compensation policies, and territory or customer ownership issues.

First, this chapter will examine this "old" dynamic of channel partner relationships, noting its inadequacy, as it leads to ineffective campaigns, decreased sales and aggravated partner relationships. Then, it will examine current shifts in the traditional business partner dynamic. Ultimately, the chapter will provide insight by illuminating and carefully detailing how industry leaders are improving partner relationships in a new and competitive landscape.

## The Situation

In the "good old days" companies such as IBM built a ubiquitous brand with unique products and then dictated their terms and funds to sales channels. Brand advertising was typically done on one of the three major TV networks, aimed at the mass market to create a "pull" that would have customers do whatever it took to get those products regardless of price, location or availability.

Product marketing teams would assemble sales and marketing material, and route it to partners via partner portals, or directly to their offices assuming that the partner had everything necessary to sell the company's products or services. And that worked, especially with those partners who were former employees.

Business was stable and predictable, but eventually the tides began to shift. The proliferation of new channels made it harder to reach and influence key customers, the window of having a truly unique product shortened, and partners started gaining a greater choice of products to recommend with various incentive programs. Gradually power over the ultimate transaction was shifting further down the value chain, thereby leaving companies with less influence over the point of sale. As a result, partners, now armed with options and leverage, became less willing to cooperate with the demands of manufacturers.

In response, manufacturers began exploring mechanisms to realign themselves as key influencers and discovered the following:

- Inconsistencies in communication about marketing programs, incentives, service and who owned the customer left partners confused and frustrated.
- Partners felt as if they were receiving little to no marketing support from manufacturers, despite having piles of marketing material and funds.
- A concerning trend was developing in which partners began using less and less of the marketing development funds (MDF) available to them.

Given these observations, it became clear that the old "push" product and programs through partners and "pull" customers to your products through mass marketing was no longer working. It was time to rethink the model.

## The Collaborative Partner Model

The new collaborative partner model begins with an organization moving beyond one-way marketing communication with their partner to a relationship consisting of a deeper engagement; instead of pushing three-ring binders out the door, companies that use the new partner model create processes that incorporate feedback loops and mechanisms for collecting partner input. The result is a better partner relationship and improved program performance.

This new partner-friendly marketing "ecosystem" helps organizations remain competitive and connected. The goal is to establish a kinetic system that allows for the real-time flow of information between companies, partners, and customers, resulting in programs and campaigns that move away from episodic one-way directed communications to being aligned, relevant, timely and "on demand."

Additionally, constant monitoring of this closed environment provides marketers with real time information on the effectiveness of offers and campaigns, the impact of key messages and value propositions, and the ability to make quick changes to programs as they are executed.

> "The goal is to establish a kinetic system that allows for the real-time flow of information between companies, partners and customers..."

## Constructing the New Model

Recent research into the high tech industry provided a roadmap for this evolution. Specifically, these ten critical areas were identified as starting points for establishing dynamic and successful partner relationships for any business.

| Area of Opportunity | Improvement Recommendations |
|---|---|
| Marketing & Sales Planning | Involve partners in the planning process. As an example, HP has a small and medium business (SMB) segment advisory council that includes 15 partners from across the U.S. Members meet frequently to develop partner programs and give feedback to HP on their SMB channel strategy. |
| Marketing Database | Allow partners to access or create queries: Microsoft found that despite churning out numerous marketing programs, many were not being executed by partners. After realizing that one of the main reasons for this inefficiency was that they lacked a quality database of targets, Microsoft responded by allowing partners to build prospect lists by leveraging its marketing database. |
| Campaign Design | Collaborate with partners on campaign design, the customer value proposition, and offers: The increase in services revenue has forced partners to become increasingly vertically aligned. As a result, they have become extremely knowledgeable about, and attuned to, customer needs, particularly in the SMB segment. |
| Resource Support | Provide more than financial support to partners: Cloud computing is highlighting a new group of potential partners, namely independent software developers (ISVs). ISVs, unlike well-established partners such as value added resellers and distributors, are generally small and lack internal support resources. As a result, their needs vary widely in particular, their operational support, such as HR, Marketing and Training, is often limited. |
| Lead Segmentation & Scoring | Involve partners in defining and scoring leads: Partners have commented that they often have different views and opinions on what makes a qualified lead. Even the definition of "lead" was inconsistent across partners and vendors. This lack of basic common language creates misalignment of priorities, tension between sales and marketing and most unfortunately, missed and even dropped opportunities. |
| Lead Management | Provide support for follow-up and lead management: Vendors should not only provide a partner relationship management system (PRM), but also, the additional resource support, such as telemarketing to help partners follow up on leads. HP's Alliance One partner program provides partners with a lead management program called Lead Lifecycle Management, provided by vendor Market One. |

| Area of Opportunity | Improvement Recommendations, cont. |
|---|---|
| Marketing Budgets & Funding | Help partners spend their marketing development funds (MDF or Contra): Failure to spend available marketing dollars causes frustration for both vendors and partners alike. Research has pinpointed that this commonly occurs because of frustration with the process to acquire funding and/or the lack of time, expertise and resources to execute programs. Manufacturers are now enabling their partners by building programs and campaigns that they can execute on behalf of partners. |
| System Support | Improve partners' access and use of important tools, systems and infrastructure: Cisco has invested $1 billion in infrastructure support and training in addition to their operating budgets. Avaya, has developed a version of their customer database that partners can license at a discount through Saleforce.com. |
| Training | Create continuous and tiered training programs: "Partner Empower" is a program designed to help Motorola better support evolving customer needs through a focus on specialization and certification. The new program tracks will include opportunities for certification in key areas, along with the opportunity to earn designation as a "Partner Empower Specialist" or "Elite Specialist." |
| Communication | Be consistent and coordinated in communications to the channel: Partners repeatedly mention their frustrations with vendor communication. Frequently, the identified issues revolve around inconsistency and frequency of message. Intel's Software Partner Program had a difficult time attracting and communicating with developers, so they created an integrated communication platform that linked a dozen corporate blogs with social media channels such as Facebook, LinkedIn and Twitter. |

## CASE STUDY
## Avaya: Driving Better Business Performance Through Deeper Engagement

**The Client.** Avaya is a global leader in enterprise communications systems providing unified communications, contact centers, data solutions and related services worldwide through its channel partners.

**The Challenge.** Prior to the recession, many of Avaya's partners were too sales-centric, focusing almost exclusively on chasing opportunity at the cost of their marketing knowledge and ability. The increasing pressures of the recession in late December 2007 began drying up pipelines and lengthening sales cycles, ultimately translating into fewer and smaller deals that required more opportunity and investment. Simultaneously, the recession impacted vendors, slowing their demand engines and causing them to hand over fewer leads to their partners.

Because of their traditional focus on converting, rather than creating demand, Avaya's partners lacked an understanding of how to effectively manage customer accounts, nurture relationships, build awareness, and create new opportunity by marketing their business services and solutions. Not only did they lack the marketing insight to generate demand, but partners also lacked the marketing tools, resources, and skill sets to market, sell, and deliver their solutions.

According to Patti Moran, Senior Director of worldwide channel marketing at Avaya, 90 percent of their channel partners lacked a dedicated marketing support person in-house. Noting this dire situation, Moran contends that ultimately "it's not enough to just be a sales organization. To be successful at growing and adapting to the market condition, partners have to have a marketing function."

**The Solution.** Recognizing the need to educate, train, and arm its partners with the necessary materials and resources to remain competitive, Avaya created a series of global workshops with distributors, titled *Marketing Masterclass,* to educate and provide resources and tools to enable small and midsized partners. During the workshops, Avaya helped the partners evaluate their strengths and weaknesses, allowing them to better understand how to position and differentiate themselves in competitive markets.

To continue the momentum generated by the workshops, Avaya created an education curriculum program, providing partners with "How to" guides, covering marketing topics ranging from writing marketing plans to building websites and leverage social media. Finally, Avaya developed a spectrum of shared services to support partners' marketing efforts, both full-service and self-service.

**The Implementation.** The first set of guides focused on key topics such as the corporate brand, instilling a long-term relationship-based sales approach, marketing's role in building client relationships, as well as growing and defending key customer accounts, information partners needed to drive their own demand.

In addition to this support, Avaya also enabled partners by providing access to supporting services, databases, events, content, and pre-existing templates and prebuilt product pages for free or at a highly discounted price. For example, Avaya created a self-service "Partner Marketing Central" portal that provides free and easy-to-use e-mail blast technology, seminars and white papers, and access to over 200 customizable marketing materials with a full range of media. Avaya also created "MarketLeaders," a full service campaign program that delivers integrated campaigns with end-to-end support. The program's intent is to achieve a range of goals in areas of relationship management, demand generation and customer engagement with the impact of enabling partners to use market development funds (MDF) or business development funds (BDF) to drive leads, nurture relationships and build awareness.

Financially, Avaya sought to ease its partners' cash flow concerns and increase their speed to market by invoicing and debiting against their funds rather than insisting partners pay up front.

**The Results.** The success of Avaya's efforts, characterized by full classes, newly engaged partners, and efficient MDF and BDF spending, has been met by requests from partners for even more education and support. Indeed, specific user feedback highlights Avaya's programs, saving partners' time and money and adding valuable sales to their pipelines. Furthermore, the global breadth and overall extent of participation speak volumes to Avaya's success — and because of this success, components have been provided in multiple languages and various offerings. For example, the self-service Partner Central has been used by over 2,500 worldwide members to create over 33,000 highly customized and targeted marketing materials. In addition, in the Americas alone, more than 1,200 partner companies have taken advantage of the MarketLeaders campaigns to generate over 1,950 of their own strategic campaigns.

Ultimately Avaya's efforts represent a prime example of how the creation of a collaborative model that provides partners the requisite tools, knowledge and resources will lead to a deeper engagement that drives better business performance.

**R. Scott Gillum** is a senior vice president with GyroHSR and leads the Channel Marketing practice based in Washington, DC. Prior to joining GyroHSR, Scott spent over twelve years with MarketBridge, a leading sales and marketing consulting firm, helping clients build, manage and optimize their business partner channels. Scott is a noted B2B author and blogger. His work on integrated sales and marketing pipelines was the subject of a Harvard Business Review case study. GyroHSR has been a member of BMA Colorado since 2007.

# 15 | Ensuring Marketing Success Through Strategic Execution

Laurie Lavelle

The high-level goals were developed; those goals were translated into brilliant marketing strategy; and the plan looked fantastic on paper — so what went wrong? To sum it up in one very powerful word: execution! All your hard work on the marketing strategy and plan ended up falling short due to limited or no effort put into the execution strategy and plan. One key question to ask yourself, "Did you give enough thought to enabling the three most critical areas for successful execution: your *people*, *processes* and *tools*?" Whether you're top-level management, in the middle, or working the fine details of marketing, this chapter is dedicated to helping connect the critical execution side of marketing through operations and enablement to the equally critical front-end strategy and planning side ensuring total success of your marketing.

*"Execution is a discipline. People think of execution as the tactical side of business. That's the first big mistake. Tactics are central to execution, but execution is not tactics. Execution is fundamental to strategy and has to shape it. No worthwhile strategy can be planned without taking into account the organization's ability to execute it."* (Larry Bossidy and Ram Charon, 2002).

Marketing operations and enablement are not typically taught in our college marketing programs, and very little is done in continued education, even though the complexity of our marketing world has gone up considerably in the last decade. Trends include globalization, remote or virtual teams, new media, and myriad technologies, to name a few. In addition, there is the ongoing challenge of finding and keeping top talent in our agencies and in-house marketing teams. According to many business process management (BPM) experts, 85 percent of all organizational problems can be attributed to processes, and the remaining 15 percent usually falls into the people category.[1]

As marketers we must look at all sides of the equation and ensure that we're not only being creative geniuses, but also being superior business people driving efficient and effective operations and results — whether as an agency or in-house department.

## Steps to Enablement

To get started, here are a few easy steps to help you start thinking from a marketing operations and enablement standpoint.

1. **Define the requirements.** First, define and clearly understand the operational challenges to accomplishing the strategy you're creating. Ditch the blinders, the status-quo "we can't" attitudes and obstacles, and enumerate what you need (your business requirements) to get the job accomplished. Create a list. It can be high-level at first, but eventually get to a comprehensive list of business requirements and rank them as to importance.

2. **Find the gaps.** After you've gone through the exercise of understanding your business requirements, it's time to map them back to reality. This is where the rubber meets the road. You'll need to take an aggressive approach to identify any gaps between the requirements and your current resources: *people*, *processes*, and *tools*. Add these items to your list in another column so you can clearly analyze them. In addition, add a scoring system so you know the importance of the identified gap. For instance, a simple red, yellow, green scheme could be followed. This type of scoring system can also help you identify the risk inherent in each gap (i.e., if this particular gap is not addressed and solved, it would be a high risk to the success of the marketing strategy). And, if you're very aggressive, add a column for cost/price as well, so you can have all your information in one place.

3. **Analyze and close the gaps.** Analyze your scoring system and identify critical gaps. At this point you should start adding in the costs of closing the gaps.

4. **Create the plan:** After the business requirements have been listed and the gaps have been identified, analyzed and solved, it's time to create the execution side of your plan. This is the other half of the strategy. Whereas you've identified the "what" in relation to marketing segmentation/target-

ing, campaigns, etc., now it's time to apply the "how" on getting it done. This step involves developing new processes, revising existing processes, adding new tools and adjusting job responsibilities.

5. **Monitor, adjust, improve.** Once the plan is set into motion it's critical to monitor it and make needed adjustments in order to continually improve it. For instance, is that new process you or your team designed working? Is the new tool that was implemented working according to plan? Is the new job responsibility that was added to the mix getting done, and is the change effective? It sounds simple enough, but as marketers we're all busy and guilty of the "set and forget" mentality. Avoid this mistake. Pay as much attention to the monitoring and the follow-up on the marketing operations and enablement side as you would to the customer messaging side of your strategy.

> "As marketers we must look at all sides of the equation and ensure that we're not only being creative geniuses, but also being superior business people..."

By following these five simple steps you can help eliminate much drama and emotion while getting into facts and data very quickly. This basic formula was applied in the following business case study and assisted greatly in moving the conversation away from strictly people and headcount into other directions to meet very important business goals.

## CASE STUDY
## Using a Marketing Operations and Enablement Approach

**The Challenge.** The in-house marketing services team had a goal set by the corporation's executive team to increase their output. Since they were a revenue-generating entity of the overall business, they were tasked to increase their revenue and specifically their profit by approximately 30 percent without increasing their headcount or overall operational costs.

The senior management team of the marketing services group was pulled into an emergency meeting where the high-level financial goals were presented by the director. Several of the management team immediately threw their hands in the air and declared defeat. The common response was that without additional headcount there was no way the team could obtain the goals that had been put forth by upper management. However, the bottom line was they did not have a choice and needed to figure out how to get it done. The department director knew this goal had to be accomplished and did not want to lose any valued employees in the process.

**The Solution.** Instead of asking, or begging, executive management for more staff, the marketing services senior leadership team took an operational and process-oriented approach to solving the problem.

First, a high-level business requirements list was created. Then critical gaps were identified, which primarily related to people's time and the types of projects they worked on (not the people themselves). Next, processes and the tools to assist and automate them were examined. This all led to a deep-dive analysis of the following areas:

### Analysis of all Job Types
- Job complexity and hours required led to a leveling of all jobs with a score being assigned to each
- Additional scoring was given for revenue and profit generated by Job Type
- Based on the Job Type Scores, the team mapped the resources required to do the different types of jobs.
- The lowest level Job Type was then analyzed to see if there were less expensive outside resources that could produce the work instead of the more expensive, highly skilled internal team members. The outcome was positive in this respect, because 25 percent of the jobs could be outsourced for less expense while freeing the internal staff to take on more revenue-generating, higher-profit activities to help meet the financial goal.

### Analysis of tools and processes
- As a result of the Job Type and Scoring exercise, several new fields were added to the already existing department Job Tracking System. This allowed for a more automated, systematic method of entering in the Job Type Scores, staffing assignments (especially helpful when certain types of jobs were outsourced), tracking, and reporting.
- Several new processes were developed to hand off lower-level Job Types to outside resources. These processes included clear documentation and overview information to accompany the job,

confidentiality agreements and proper contracts created for all outsourced individuals and companies, timeline expectations, and delivery methods.

- A tool was implemented for easy collaboration between internal management and the outsourced talent. The tool used was Microsoft's SharePoint program due to the low cost required to add outsourced users in a secure environment. (Other tools considered were Aquent's Robohead and Apple's iWork.com tool.) SharePoint enabled a smooth review, collaboration and approval workflow process. E-mail was eliminated immediately as a workflow tool due to large file sizes and clumsy archive and retrieval capabilities.
- Quarterly review processes were developed to score the outsourced model which included both scoring of internal processes and the performance of the outside resources doing the work. A simple but very effective score card was developed which made the process consistent and repeatable.

**The Results.** The financial goal was not only met, but exceeded. The team was able to add the additional revenue and exceeded the profit goal and hit almost 40 percent. Due to the Job Type and Scoring system, the team was able to free up considerable time for the internal resources, which were able to work on the bigger, more profitable jobs. Additionally, more resources could focus on bringing in additional business. And, because the quality of the work went up considerably, additional business was gained from existing clients.

Another result from the Job Type and Scoring system was the ability to meet with executive management and provide factual data, versus the approach used in the past that relied on more anecdotal information. The ability to show how and why the financial goals were met and exceeded was a first for this division and added credibility to the department in the eyes of executive and C-level management.

---

Bossidy, Larry and Ram Charan. Execution — *The Discipline of Getting Things Done*. Crown Publishing Group, Random House, 2002.

[1] Madison, Dan. *Process Mapping, Process Improvement, and Process Management: A Practical Guide to Enhancing Work and Information Flow*. Paton Press, 2005.

 **Laurie Lavelle**, CBC, owner/principal of Greenfield Marketing Group, LLC has almost 20 years of corporate B2B marketing strategy, marketing communications, and marketing operations experience in addition to an MBA in marketing. Her career started in design and visual communication and then progressed into marketing management within two global Fortune 200 and 100 corporations, working with the largest brand names in technology. This background gave her a clear understanding of the blend between the art and science of marketing. As a recent business owner of a small B2B consultancy, Laurie has been able to combine her experience into a unique focus on marketing operations enablement and project management. Laurie has been a very active member of BMA for over a decade, earning her CBC and holding various positions on the BMA Colorado chapter board of directors.

# 16 | Using PR 2.0 to Increase Your Brand's Competitive Edge

Yann Ropars

Much of the social media buzz these days focuses on the free tools available to all of us. Things have been simplified so much with Facebook and Twitter, it's easy to think that these tools are all you need. But in a B2B environment, getting social media right is essential, or it's just a waste of time. If your company is considering starting, or improving, a social media program, now is a good time to reflect on what you're doing and why you're doing it at all. Hanging out on social networks is not enough, no matter what your budget. You need to make something happen: You need PR 2.0.

PR 2.0 stands for Public Relations 2.0, which is the sum of online conversations and their associated "resonance" between brands and their constituents. Of course it is best to have positive and robust resonance around your brand to increase its value. It should be noted that PR 2.0 does not need a marketing department to exist. It is accomplished through the sheer amount of information exchanged about a brand, its products, people, practices and brand behavior. The role of PR 2.0 strategies is to harness the positive, learn from the negative, and provide a gathering place that will keep constituents engaged, empowered and ready to transact/interact.

This chapter addresses three important components of the PR 2.0 environment: Why you should invest in a PR 2.0 strategy; where to aim for success; and how to incorporate it with traditional efforts. This chapter is for strategic thinkers and implementers alike.

## Why a PR 2.0 Approach

Let's start with numbers as they speak a certain truth: 500 million users in five years on Facebook; 150 million handles/users on Twitter and its status as the fastest growing search engine; 60 million users on LinkedIn; and, 130 million blogs. In 2010, 23 percent of time spent on the Internet was spent on social networks, up from 16 percent in 2009.[1] We create more information every couple of days than we created from the dawn of humanity through to 2003 (Eric Schmidt, Google CEO). The amount of online noise is certainly proportionally as high, which creates a superb opportunity to stand out through quality.

**PR 2.0 is about resonance.** Businesses that adopt these communication methods and venues en masse can influence and be influenced because social media users are more influential than the average population. Their information-sharing behaviors are viral with media power-like abilities to spread the word. They produce and share more information than traditional networks. Moreover, this new world is measured by "resonance" — the number of times a piece of content is viewed, shared, liked, or promoted on social networks. Online newspapers know this very well, as an increasing portion of their traffic comes from social network referrals. People will only repeat stories — create marketing resonance — if they can make other people connect to those stories. Through these repetitions, new marketing messages come alive outside the control of the PR and marketing departments.

New media is also powered by the crowd to take the message and spin up or dial down its information. Resonance is created in and through four constituencies: 1) Internal staff, 2) Customers, 3) Prospects, 4) Industry influencers. Having these constituencies active and interactive builds your brand as a conversational hub. Unfortunately, a Facebook fan page and Twitter account alone will not make this happen, especially if you use them like broadcast media.

**The Four Constituencies**

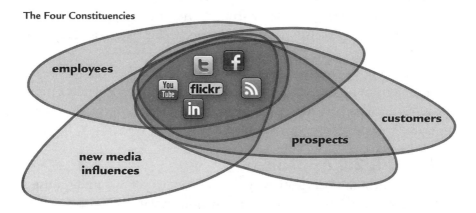

## What About Goals for Success

In B2B, it's always about conversion. Conversion is making someone act in favor of your business by generating traffic, getting a new client, purchasing services or getting recommended. Marketing generates leads. Sales closes deals. It's cut and dried. With PR 2.0, numbers are never the priority (although many measures are available to track such numbers, unlike traditional PR). Building relationships is the key. So getting constituent buy-in, affection and engagement are the top priorities. Those you engage will spread the word and micro-market your brand and product for you. Most companies look to Facebook and Twitter to simply have plenty of fans and followers. But, that's too simple, and if you're in that game, you're most likely in the B2C environment. As stated before, relationships are the key, even though they are not that easy to create and sustain.

> "With PR 2.0, numbers are never the priority. ... Building relationships is the key."

As marketers, we're presented with choices — short-term vs. long-term, spikes or gradual growth. At one end of the spectrum, companies have short sales cycles and brands are mostly transactional. A mix of advertising and social network promotional campaigns, operating separately but side by side, may be a good strategy. At the other end of the spectrum, your sales cycles might be longer and your brand, experiential, or perhaps your brand's trust is a very important component of your marketing strategy. In this case, an integrated PR 2.0 program using a mix of cohesive offline and online engaging strategies for identification, not lead generation, is right for you. Advertising may still be useful here to bring customer awareness to your social presence.

As stated before, B2B marketing is all about conversion. In the best case scenario, your Web analytics feed your customer relationship management (CRM)/sales module system and you can link social media activities with sales. In most cases, though, you'll be able to harvest a ton of clicks and behavioral interests about your constituency and customers. Integration is, however, being forged between Google Analytics, landing pages and your CRM software. This data is very important as you can accurately measure improvements which other marketing avenues, advertising for example, may not always offer. One should be aware that companies with a high branding budget will have an easier time showing high numbers. These companies rarely do a better job at engaging their constituency, however.

## How Can We Become a Conversational Brand

### Pull 2/3: Push 1/3

A customer service mindset is the best way to describe the skills needed for those leading your social media effort. Remember, those whom you seek to resonate with (spread your word) will do so because they believe in something beyond the transactional relationship. Push marketing is defined as a traditional broadcast, one-way method where the receiver has no ability to comment or respond, e.g., advertising, pay-per-click, etc. *Pull marketing*, on the other hand, is the art of marketing your constituents' news and achievements without making the story about your own brand. For example, someone tweets about their experience purchasing a pair of shoes at an online store. The brand manager picks it up, retweets the original tweet, which creates a flurry of other tweets and retweets, thus building the buzz around the brand. As you grow into the skill of pulling, your brand will become a conversational hub. Mixing push and pull marketing activities across your networks then becomes second nature. If you don't balance your push/pull activities, you'll quickly become irrelevant and unnoticed in the stream of those who matter to your business. Using your intuition — would you send this tweet to a friend? — is a good way of gauging your alignment with your constituencies.

### The Reverse Funnel Strategy

Traditional B2B marketing strategies create a downward funnel of activities that ultimately translate into leads and closed sales. Within the PR 2.0 frame, this process damages the relationships you're trying to target. Adopting the same sales funnel techniques with social media is seen as abusing the relationship. Instead, reach out to your core constituents and work with them. All those who participate with your brand, products or services across platforms need to be identified and studied with programs put in place to augment their engagement. They have the potential to create a multiplier effect. It doesn't matter whether it's a customer tweeting about your brand or a Google-search organic referral; all resonance agents will act in your favor if your words and actions are relevant. In transforming traditional marketing to PR 2.0, being relevant is the toughest task for any brand. Remember, your aim is to become a conversational hub, not to push a message. The conversation may not always be directly relevant to you. It should, instead, serve the interests that your constituents or communities have in common. It's always about making your content, touch points and conversations relevant to others.

**The Sales vs. Social Media Funnel**

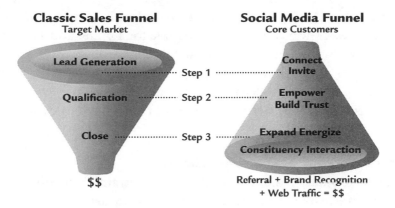

Social media users have proven to be more influential than regular folks. They speak about their product and service experiences, write Web reviews, make comments on blogs, etc. Sharing and influencing is a part of their life. PR 2.0 tactics help find them, engage them and care for them — making them a positive viral asset to your community(ies).

## Value Chain: You're Part of It

Calibrating your activities to achieve resonance is a complex endeavor. Every person or brand is part of an information eco system. To be successful, you have to look at your entire value chain and its participants in creating a proper social media strategy. Your company is not the only thing that matters, but all those upstream and downstream as well. Becoming an information and conversation hub is a great challenge that can only be overcome if you consider most of your constituents as part of your social media activities. You'll be speaking with customers, prospects, influencers and others.

## Build Your Stories and Resource Your Program

Engaging constituents starts with telling stories and adding value to them. The issue is whether internal resources or external resources, like agencies, are the best to take care of those tasks. Internal "un-conferences" — brown bag lunches or open style gatherings — will get staff volunteers to engage the groundswell ideals an organization needs to be successful with social media. A customer-services mind is often required to successfully manage a social network community. Marketers are usually extroverts. Installing patterns of two-way conversation usually necessitates some introversion. Remember, you are here to serve the constituents. Egocentric and pushy behaviors have little place in social media. *Listen, and listen well.* New media makes it possible for a brand and a company to become a news outlet hub. Crowdsourcing through constituents is necessary to be successful. Managing and encouraging those activities is where the marketing department should be focusing. And yes, the department should be slowly releasing control as it educates others.

## Integrate Your Marketing Channels

Social media and PR 2.0, by themselves, are certainly not sufficient for a successful marketing campaign. Brand constituents are affected in offline and online ways. It is very important that your PR 2.0 strategy takes into account all constituency touch points. As you integrate PR 2.0 aspects into your marketing mix, you are allowing a two-way exchange of information. In some ways, it's like crowdsourcing the messaging and loosening the control. Educate your four constituencies in online behavior and encourage them to participate, engaging in meaningful ways.

Every offline marketing activity should create a two-stage call to action: Connect with the brand and make people feel comfortable participating. For example, always refer to your twitter handle on brochures (e.g. http://twitter.com/yannr). Refresh all your marketing assets to invite interaction, not just transaction. When you send employees to conferences, also send "micro-journalists" to take photos, share news and post relevant information. There are plenty of online tools available to harvest content and interactions. Smartphone devices are often the best way to start creating simple, yet very visible, content. Posterous.com group features, for example, allow many authorized members to create meaningful content, which can then be used to engage constituents. Slowly, traditional marketing tactics will interweave with the new ones. Some will disappear as they yield neither monetary nor social currency rewards, and that's OK.

## CASE STUDY
## The Neenan Company

**The Client.** The Neenan Company (TNC) is a B2B design-build and construction firm specializing in architecture and construction for schools, health care, government and other commercial facilities. The Neenan Company's culture is very participatory and progressive in nature and a large reason why it leads the industry when it comes to social media.

**The Challenge.** The company wanted to increase its nationwide visibility in its niche market, as much of the business generated is usually done through long-term trusted relationships and sales cycles. PR efforts from the past had not yielded expected results. Could PR 2.0 allow Neenan to create a new form of digital asset and marketing continuum matching their business culture?

**The Discovery.** The conversation started in late 2008 with a few executives, but was put on hold till mid-2009 when a group of employees brought Extanz in for a discovery session. There was much debate about the value of an integrated program over other marketing methods. But with a nationwide reach and client base, a PR 2.0 approach made sense.

**The Solution.** From a single website with no Internet strategy, The Neenan Company opted for a three-prong program recommended by Extanz which would include guest blogging, social network engagement and new-media influencer outreach.

**The Implementation.** The Neenan Company social media and PR 2.0 program was designed and launched in late 2009, embarking on the transformational journey to becoming a conversational brand. Beyond implementing social media tools, its Internet visibility increased in terms of opening up to its larger constituency and facilitating conversations across social networks involving its four different constituencies. The implementation has not been without struggle, however. Everyone in the organization has an opinion, yet inviting the wider participation of employees is increasingly critical to their current success, so employee surveys have become essential to "internal crowdsourcing" and feedback for the program. Nurturing these programs constantly is also necessary, like building any good relationship, and The Neenan Company social media and PR 2.0 program has evolved alongside their constituency's capacity for engagement. Increasing numbers of community members now blog formally as well as act as journalists for the many events they attend. In their second year of the program, The Neenan Company's social media personality continues to evolve and grow, as do their relationships and communities, guided by insights from key data points of PR 2.0. For a very analytical, yet collaborative-learning company like TNC, this partnering PR 2.0 strategy has proven a tangible success.

**The Results.** The Neenan Company has enjoyed a 300 percent increase in traffic compared to its first year. Every activity it engages in supports its visibility and community: search engine rankings and referrals, blog comments, Internet referrals, external article mentions, social network mentions, and placements to Twitter mentions. The social media program has increased Web traffic and opened opportunities to build new partnerships. By default, the program also supports lead generation efforts even though it may not show a direct correlation, given the length of The Neenan Company's sales cycle.

## Conclusion

Much of the social media buzz these days focuses on the free tools available to all of us. But in a B2B environment, getting social media right using an array of tools is essential because of the focus on relationships. A PR 2.0 approach enables you to create resonance around your brand by harnessing the energy and wisdom of your core constituencies — employees, customers, prospects and influencers — and then creating a gathering place to keep them engaged, empowered and ready to transact/interact. Exploring a PR 2.0 strategy, deciding on which goals you will use to measure success, and then working to turn your brand into a conversational hub is the work of strategic thinkers and implementers across your organization, not just in your marketing and PR departments.

---

[1] http://www.businessweek.com/technology/content/aug2010/tc2010081_994774.htm

 **Yann Ropars**, originally from France, moved to Colorado in 1999 to finish his MBA at the University of Colorado/Denver through the University of Diepenbeek in Belgium. He has worked in marketing and business development for the last ten years in the United States, New Zealand and France. Yann jumped into the social media space in 2006 and now runs Extanz.com, an agency focused on PR 2.0 and inbound marketing. He joined BMA Colorado in 2010.

# 17 | Inbound Lead Generation and Marketing Automation Strategies

Michael Ward

A dvances in marketing technology are enabling B2B marketers to deliver relevant messaging at an increasingly granular level, and the results are impressive. Marketing automation — a collection of behavioral monitoring, lead scoring and lead nurturing technologies — is predicted to see large-scale adoption in the coming years due to both the efficacy and efficiency with which it drives revenue.

Getting the most from the latest technology often begins with an understanding of not only how, but also why, it works so well. In this chapter we'll take a look at one of the concepts driving innovation in B2B marketing technology as well as the capabilities afforded by these innovations. We'll wrap up with a brief case study illustrating the successful use of the latest and greatest.

## The One Word Business Plan: What Truly Works in Marketing

There's a single word that guides nearly every conversation you have. It's there when you speak with your spouse, your children, your friends and co-workers. It's a natural part of normal human conversation, making it more effective and helping to build lasting relationships.

This word is also the foundation of many business interactions. Every deal that gets closed has this word to thank. This word is responsible for the popularity of both Google's search engine and the success of their core revenue generator, AdWords. The word is "relevance": It is the difference between success and failure in marketing. It's also the driver behind many of the technological innovations gaining a foothold in B2B marketing today.

We've all heard that art imitates life. Technology regularly imitates life, as well. Enterprising people often use technology not to create a new process or task of their invention, but rather to add efficiency and scale to a process or task performed every day. Marketing automation fits this description. The collection of technologies that comprise a marketing automation solution attempts to add efficiency and scale to the process used by great salespeople to get deals done and stay relevant to the needs of the prospect.

Great salespeople use relevance as their go-to tool on a daily basis. It's a simple process with two steps: listen and respond based on what you've heard, and then repeat. Great salespeople are "listening" on many levels. They hear the words the prospect says. They observe body language and pay attention to tone of voice. They watch for facial expressions and shifts of position. All of these observations help the salesperson formulate their response.

In responding, great salespeople have a wealth of knowledge and experience to draw upon. They know their product or service very well. They know the industry and are familiar with the competition and their products, tactics and pricing. A great salesperson can choose, at any given moment, from a whole host of responses in conversation. For a great salesperson, the choice is clear: choose the response most relevant to the needs expressed by the prospect at hand.

**Relevance works.** It works when you talk to your spouse about tonight's dinner. It works when your coworker asks about the trade show schedule. It works when having a serious discussion in the boss's office or when letting loose with your friends on the weekend. It's what works in marketing, as well, and automating it is the goal of marketing automation.

Relevance is the basis of human interaction. Staying relevant to the topic at hand in a conversation or meeting is automatic for most of us. We pick up on the cues available, process them and respond without having to think about it. Staying relevant is what makes communication work. It will also work for you as a B2B marketer. But how does one communicate in a relevant manner to each lead in your database when your database contains 10,000 prospects? How about 100,000 or 1,000,000? Even 1,000 prospects is an overwhelming number when dealt with individually.

## Listen, Respond With Relevance, Repeat

> *"Marketing automation tools emulate the process of listening to prospects by monitoring the individual behavior of each prospect..."*

How significant is it when a prospect clicks a link in a marketing e-mail and visits your website? The answer, of course, depends on additional information. Who clicked the link? Was it a high-value decision maker or someone not as important to your marketing effort? On what link did they click? More importantly, what happened *after* they clicked on the link? Did the prospect look at a single page and "bounce" off your website or did they dig deeper? What specific pages did they view? Did they come back to the site for a repeat visit? What other interactions has this individual had with your brand? Is this person exhibiting behavior typical of a well-qualified lead? Do you know what behavior is typical of a well-qualified lead?

Marketing automation tools emulate the process of listening to prospects by monitoring the individual behavior of each prospect as he interacts with your website, e-mail campaigns and other online assets. They know which Web pages each lead looks at and for how long. They know which PDF files are viewed, which videos are watched and by whom. They even know which Web pages weren't viewed by a given individual. They know the search phrases used by each prospect, their general location (city, state and country) and whether it's this prospect's first or fourth visit to your site.

Behavior can be used to quantify and qualify lead interest. Obviously, the prospect that looks at a single page on your site and leaves is behaving differently, and arguably less qualified, than one that looks at twelve pages today and comes back to look at seven more tomorrow. But, behavior alone isn't enough to qualify a lead.

A marketing automation system will also connect to your customer relationship management (CRM) application and access existing leads and job titles, roles, specific geographic locations and other fields. This allows you to augment behavioral data with traditional database marketing fields such as address information, annual revenue and number of employees.

But, what's to be done with all this statistical and behavioral data? How does it combine to determine lead qualification and deliver relevant messaging? This is where "automation" comes into play.

## Lead Scoring: A Logical Next Step

When that great salesperson sizes up a lead, many factors are analyzed instantaneously: male or female; products of interest; level of interest; decision maker; ability to pay. The salesperson is able to quickly size up the prospect, determine what stage they're in and decide upon appropriate steps. Your marketing automation system must handle this sizing up for you automatically. This is a feature known as lead scoring.

A prospect's lead score is most logically broken down into three components.

1. The "Contact" score evaluates information such as job title, role and decision-making ability. The contact score also takes into account the presence of certain requisite information about the prospect, such as name, e-mail address and phone number.
2. The "Activity" score gauges how active the prospect has been on your website, blog or other digital assets, as well as e-mail click-throughs and other campaign-related activity.
3. An "Engagement" score measures the prospect's level of engagement with your company. Engagement is defined by events in which the prospect takes proactive steps to engage with your brand, such as filling out a Web form, webinar registration, online chat, free trial downloads, etc.

A prospect's interactions with your digital assets are not scored equally. Some interactions are of higher value and will have a higher impact on lead score. For example, a software company would typically assign a higher value to their licensing or pricing pages, as prospects viewing these may well be moving into a buying phase. Likewise, certain assets may have a negative buying correlation. Job seekers are often of little value as prospects. Visits to your careers page will normally have a negative impact on a prospect's lead score.

A capable lead-scoring system will automatically assign default values to certain types of interactions. E-mail click-throughs, repeat website visits and online registrations are assigned a predetermined number of points by default. You may also want to store more than one lead score per prospect. If you sell multiple products or services you may want to score prospects based on their activity and engagement with each one separately.

Lead scoring is the automated equivalent of sizing up prospects to determine their interests and stage in the buying process. With this information in hand, our great salesperson knows how to stay relevant to the prospect's needs. Automating this relevance is known as lead nurturing.

## Automated Relevance: Lead Nurturing

The dictionary definition of nurture says things like "feed and protect," "support during development" and "educate." These are the goals of any well-conceived lead-scoring campaign. Applied to marketing automation, lead-nurturing amounts to the delivery of relevant content to each prospect based on interests and on stage in the buying process. But, how does that translate into action?

A great salesperson doesn't pounce on a lead with contract terms if the prospect is asking general questions about product benefits. Nor should a marketer blast out end-of-quarter pricing discounts to every lead in their database.

Leads determined to be early in the buying process should be educated, not sold. Further, they should be educated about the benefits of products or services they have expressed interest in via their actual behaviors, including surveys, Web page views, phone conversations, etc. A lead-nurturing campaign for a prospect in this stage may consist of an automated series of e-mails delivering tips, best practices or general product information. The prospect's interaction with each of these pieces is monitored. Did they open the e-mail? Did they click-through? Did their website visit indicate that they've moved into buying mode? The lead-scoring system is watching vigilantly for all of these behaviors and can automatically move the prospect from a "research mode" campaign into a "buying mode" campaign. It can also assign the lead to the appropriate great salesperson in your CRM when the time is right.

In practice, you want to automatically set up nurturing campaigns that deliver appropriate content to prospects in various stages of the buying process. You also want your lead-scoring system to back up those campaigns so prospects flow through the system at their own pace. The net result is well-primed prospects being handed to sales with solid information about the prospects' interests and qualifications.

Much has been written about lead nurturing and the need to re-architect business processes to achieve alignment between sales and marketing in order to succeed. Many companies with limited resources are rightfully intimidated by the idea of re-engineering business processes. It would seem that a company must operate as a bureaucracy to even digest language of this nature.

Technology's advance into the world of marketing will not be stopped. A substantial competitive advantage awaits those who embrace the use of automation to qualify and nurture the warm and cold leads in their pipeline. Marketing automation doesn't have to involve an army of consultants and months of learning to be beneficial. An automated lead-scoring system, coupled with some good educational content, is enough to get started and achieve positive results.

## CASE STUDY
## Cooling Tower Depot

**The Challenge.** Cooling Tower Depot (CTD) had accumulated a database containing approximately 50,000 viable leads. CTD was unable to determine which of these prospects had needs on the near horizon and could not adequately canvas this number of prospects with their internal business development staff. They knew opportunities were being lost.

**The Client.** CTD manufactures and installs industrial cooling towers around the world. It provides repair and inspection services for existing cooling towers and sells spare parts and components as well. Its products do for industrial facilities, such as power plants and refineries, what your radiator does for your car. It cools a liquid (water) that removes heat where it must be removed for plant equipment to continue operating.

**The Journey.** CTD had augmented the efforts of their telephone-based business development personnel with occasional, undifferentiated e-mail blasts. While this resulted in some additional bidding opportunities, it was still reliant on the lucky timing of an e-mail or phone call to identify leads with pending needs. CTD had been an early adopter of Net-Results' first product, a Web-based service that identifies the companies that visit your website, and details the search phrases used and pages viewed by each prospect. When Net-Results' marketing automation product was ready for primetime, CTD was eager to make the transition.

**The Solution.** CTD maintains the most comprehensive website in the cooling tower industry. It put Net-Results lead-scoring system to work monitoring the behavior of each prospect as each interacted with the various resources made available online. Content was scored as having either high, normal or low value. Interactions indicative of engagement were given the greatest weight. This allowed the highest-value prospects to "raise their hand," in a manner of speaking.

**The Implementation.** Each of CTD's prospects generally fall into one of two categories: engineers who are involved in the design and purchase of new cooling towers, and maintenance personnel who oversee inspections, repairs and the acquisition of replacement components. CTD's database was segmented based on these two categories using job titles, past purchase/quote activity and behavioral data, where available. This enabled it to move away from undifferentiated e-mail blasts and begin nurturing prospects with content relevant to their functions and roles.

**The Results.** Leveraging existing copy from its brochures and website wherever possible, maintenance personnel now receive e-mails about cooling tower testing procedures, tips on evaluating vendor repair bids, and discounts on cooling tower parts. Engineers are nurtured with content focused on CTD's engineering expertise, industry-leading engineering tools and tips on the effective use of the various engineering resources. Prospect's interactions with this nurturing content are monitored and lead scores adjusted automatically. Leads reaching defined thresholds are passed to sales for follow-up.

The process for CTD is ongoing with additional nurturing content being added as time allows. It took about two months to get the data base segmentation in order and a moderate, but workable, amount of nurturing content in place.

*"We've been really happy with our decision to score our leads and segment our e-mail lists. Our business development personnel now focus their calling on high-value prospects based on lead score and the number of bidding opportunities they generate is up about 17 percent. Inbound leads resulting from nurturing have risen by 12 percent and we close a majority of that business."* – Michael Kast, owner, Cooling Tower Depot

**"Inbound leads resulting from nurturing have risen by 12 percent and we close a majority of that business."**

**Michael Ward** founded Net-Results Marketing Automation as an IT consulting and Web design firm in March, 2003. Shortly thereafter, Michael identified the need for companies to know who was visiting their website, why they were visiting and exactly what each high-value prospect was doing while they were there. This led Michael, a self-taught database and Web application hack, to prototype, build and launch an SaaS offering that has evolved into a full-fledged marketing automation solution used by businesses on five continents. He has been a member of BMA Colorado since 2009.

# 18 Marketing and Sales – Friends or Foes?

## Integrating the Operations and Hand-off Between Two (sometimes) Disparate Groups

Kevin Thomas

For as long as most of us can remember, the relationship between marketing and sales has been bumpy, and sometimes outright lousy. In many cases, however, it has the potential to be strong and synergistic, thus adding value on a daily basis to an organization and the individuals involved.

Why are there so many challenges? Why don't the two departments always see eye-to-eye? What can be done to help these two groups overcome their differences and join together for a common cause?

Let's take a step back and look at the personality differences between marketers and sales people. Marketing roles run the gamut from communications and research to marketing management and program/event planning, and many other roles in between. They run with campaigns and programs, creative launches and branding initiatives. The amount of testing and evaluating involved generally precludes a direct correlation to results that could translate into an immediate job loss. Sales organizations, on the other hand, generally include sales reps (both hunters and farmers), inside sales, telesales, sales operations, channel sales and support representatives. Sales teams operate on a monthly, quarterly, and annual sales and/or revenue quota. Sales is a high-risk, high-return profession and the pressure is extreme: miss your target and lose your job. But, with fame also comes fortune. There's little time for goofing off. That is not to say that marketers sit around all day with their feet up, but generally the stakes are not as high. Another view: Sales people are from Saturn, and Marketers are from Mars

## Reporting Structure

There is much debate on the reporting structure for marketing organizations. This author recently tracked a lengthy discussion on a LinkedIn group where the comments were as varied and opinionated as any discussion concerning politics or religion. The answer comes down to: It depends. It depends on the size of the company, the structure of the management team, the culture of the organization, and sometimes, the personality of the sales and marketing leaders. It also depends on the company's growth phase and the background of the senior leadership team.

> *"When a company introduces a market-focused business model, marketing needs to have a seat at the table."*

When a company introduces a market-focused business model, marketing needs to have a seat at the table. With this seat must come the autonomy to implement marketing programs and drive the marketing philosophy from the top. Conversely, there usually isn't much debate around sales' role and structure in an organization: Sales are necessary to remain in business. It's as simple as that. Sales are vital to any organization wanting to turn a profit. Thus, sales management often carries a lot of clout throughout a company and voices strong opinions on what it takes to succeed. Marketing organizations can report directly to the CEO or report into sales operations, sales, product management, public relations, or communications departments. However, the closer the reporting for these two teams, the greater the chance for success. Marketing and sales teams that report to the same senior level executive have the greatest opportunity for combined synergy, cooperation, and success.

## Goals and Desires

While the tactics and actions of each group are drastically different, the end goal is usually the same: Drive revenue. However, this is not always perceived to be true, especially for the marketers. There are many activities performed by marketers that most people in a company do not see as revenue-driving. Marketers and their functions are complex. For example, while a search engine optimization (SEO) effort does not lead directly to sales, it increases the company's exposure and "findability" on the Web, increases editorial opportunities, drives online lead efforts, and supports numerous other activities that support the sales team. While it is relatively easy to directly tie sales activity to revenue generation, in most organizations there is a good opportunity for marketing to connect the dots for their sales counterparts, thereby increasing the awareness of how marketing campaigns and activities ultimately support sales efforts and the company's goal of generating revenue.

## Systems and Tracking

There's no alternative to tracking in today's business world. In fact, most marketers and sales professionals need to sift through the endless statistics, trends, benchmarks, campaigns, touch points, responses, click-throughs, and sales results to acquire knowledge, not just for the sake of collecting information. There is Salesforce.com for sales tracking and Marketo (among many applications) for marketing automation. It is important to remember that there are two sides to these applications; the utility to manage the business and execute on tactical plans, and the back-end strategic value for making short- and long-term strategic decisions. However, our ability to truly measure the business is only as good as the data: garbage in, garbage out. Ask any marketer if they fully trust or rely on the data in their CRM tools. While you're at it, ask what they would give to jointly update and effectively manage a clean database moving forward.

The database/CRM arena is another area of great discrepancy between sales and marketing. For many sales people, these tracking and reporting systems represent a headquarter-mandated application that allows management to monitor their activity, forcing them to spend valuable time maintaining records and keeping them away from selling. There are some in sales who view applications like Salesforce.com as a modern-day Franklin Planner that allows them to focus on what's important while reminding them what to do at the appropriate time. Marketers tend to love the information and knowledge gained from any "measuring" application they can get their hands on. Speaking as a seasoned marketer, we want current information, every follow-up call, every campaign, every opened email, every online sale, every lead, and every conceivable action we can measure so we

> *"Gathering knowledge and assessing information also allows us to communicate the value marketing brings to our organizations."*

can both evaluate and modify our programs to increase our marketing and sales effectiveness. Gathering knowledge and assessing information also allows us to communicate the value marketing brings to our organizations. We want to show the company that we are not an overhead expense, but rather a revenue-driving department — especially during budgeting and headcount discussions.

Unfortunately, this insight into everyone's activities sometimes causes increased friction between sales and marketing. The key is to paint the total picture of why we collectively, as a company, value the data and what is done with the knowledge gleaned. With both parties having an understanding of the end-game, the team has a greater appreciation behind the processes and reasoning, thus reducing friction.

Even though increased awareness and automation can be a blessing for marketers, there is still this common dialog from sales: "We continue to get lousy leads from marketing and the prospect is not interested. I've called a couple of leads and I don't want to call any more until we get better leads." Marketing responds: "We are driving leads from trade shows, Web downloads, outbound marketing campaigns, and a lead-nurture program. Why should we work so hard to develop leads if sales is not going to follow-up?" Sound familiar?

## CASE STUDY
## Marketing and Sales

**The Challenge.** After years of generating leads through typical marketing and sales events, the marketing department of a large company continued to be frustrated over the large percentage of leads that were not being followed-up by sales due to lack of bandwidth and sales pipelines that were already full. Marketing knew that every touch from a tradeshow or Web form submission was not a hot lead to be an immediate follow-up by sales. However, they also knew that there may be some gems among the leads that were not being mined.

**The Client.** Marketing approached the issue focused on two types of customers: internal employees and external prospects who were interested in services. The internal customers were frustrated because they felt the leads received in the past were "cold" or not overly viable to bring into the sales pipeline yet. The external prospects "may" have a business need that could be solved, but they hadn't talked to a sales representative to make that determination.

**The Journey.** The marketing department investigated numerous options that were reasonable for the business, both from a process and budgetary perspective. Do they hire the staff in-house or outsource the project? What systems would they use to track and manage? Where would they start on the reassignment of leads? All this had to be in place before anyone pulled the trigger so marketing could hit the ground running and gain the maximum benefit from their efforts.

**The Discovery.** Through the marketing department's research, it found that the optimal situation was to utilize an expert who specialized in outbound telemarketing. His focus, systems, behavior and personality were best suited to professionally nurture their database.

**The Solution.** An outside lead-nurture and prospecting company/individual that specializes in lead nurturing was hired and trained with a focus on targeted vertical markets pulled from Salesforce.com.

**The Implementation.** Marketing took the house lists and pushed them into an outbound calling program intended to nurture the prospect to a point of genuine interest. These prospects were subsequently transferred in Salesforce.com to a company sales rep who was given five days to "claim" the lead. If a lead was not claimed, it was transferred to channel partners in Salesforce.com for the appropriate sales activity.

**The Results.** While not perfect, the program became a win-win for all concerned. The interested prospect received the information he was looking for to make a timely decision, the sales rep had the opportunity to manage the prospect if they had the bandwidth, and the channel partner received valuable pre-qualified leads if sales did not claim the lead first. Follow-up rates increased, new sales resulted from the program, and the interdepartmental teamwork between marketing, sales, and channels benefited.

## Communication

Building a strong relationship between the sales and marketing teams is all about communication. The relationship needs to be managed at all levels in the organization. It is important that at the VP level there is a respect and common vision on the ultimate goal and tactics needed for success. Equally important are the working relationships throughout each department. An open line of communication from the field sales team, where constructive input and direction are both solicited and welcomed, is vital to a marketing team. At the end of the day, the success of the sales rep is the success of the marketing team, and every other department in the organization. Intermap found that marketing individuals who attend bi-weekly sales meetings not only gather insight from the field sales teams, but also have the opportunity to directly communicate with the field staff on marketing programs, special promotions and other activities coming down the pipeline.

This chapter began by asking if sales and marketing are friends or foes. The answer is: It's up to us. Why not be colleagues who are on the same team, with the same objectives, goals, dreams, and aspirations? It beats the alternative. Sales and marketing may be from different planets, but both sides want, and need, to achieve success — for ourselves and our companies.

**Kevin Thomas** is a leader with 25 years marketing and sales operations experience in entrepreneur-based high-growth technology companies. He is a results-driven marketing leader with extensive experience delivering marketing activities that result in brand recognition and revenue contribution for companies. Educated at the University of Nevada — Reno, where he worked through college as a blackjack dealer, he began his marketing career in San Francisco before coming to Denver in the late 1990s during the telecommunications boom. He is past vice president of global marketing for Intermap Technologies, a GIS mapping company. He became a member of BMA Colorado in 2010.

# 19 | Best Practices for Sales Enablement

Cheryl Ader Smith and Lisa Haldeman

Organizations need to ensure that investments in sales enablement are delivering value to the sales force. Based on hundreds of interviews with sellers, Leopard Communications developed a series of best practices to help companies deliver more effective sales enablement programs by better aligning marketing and sales initiatives, improving sales productivity and driving sales conversation relevance with customers. This chapter will focus on three sales-enablement best practices.

Getting the most from the latest technology often begins with an understanding of not only how, but also why, it works so well. In this chapter we'll take a look at one of the concepts driving innovation in B2B marketing technology as well as the capabilities afforded by these innovations. We'll wrap up with a brief case study illustrating the successful use of the latest and greatest.

## What is Effective Sales Enablement?

Before discussing best practices for sales-enablement programs, it's important to establish that this isn't a discussion of collateral materials or data sheets or PowerPoint presentations. Sales enablement encompasses a significant number of planning, development and deployment initiatives. According to Forrester Research: "Sales enablement is a strategic, ongoing process that equips all client-facing employees with the ability to consistently and systematically have a valuable conversation with the right set of customer stakeholders at each stage of the customer's problem-solving life cycle to optimize the return of investment of the selling system."[1]

Based on Forrester's definition, sales enablement can include a wide range of marketing and sales activities and initiatives that help address the problem-solving life cycle of customers. These activities are vast and may include sales and customer research, process alignment, internal communications for sales, sales training, and tool development. Our definition of a sales-enablement program includes four core components: communications; education and training; tool development and delivery; and measurement.

- **Communications** refers to how the sales force is informed about the sales-enablement program. An effective communications plan should consistently inform the sales force about what tools and information are available and the benefits that can be realized from using them.
- **Education and training** is focused on how to successfully access and use the components of the sales-enablement program. This generally is integrated with processes and training that already exists within the client's organization.
- **Tool development and delivery** includes the assets created to help the sales force address customer needs with the offerings they represent. Assets may range from selling guides and product sheets to ROI tools and case studies. Delivery refers to the method for getting the tools in the hands of the sales force. Today, delivery has become a sophisticated initiative because the deployment and management of assets has become more complex. Digital deployment methods have been successful at managing this complexity. These methods vary greatly and can include portals, internal websites, and even mobile delivery.
- **Measurement** includes any approach to assessing the use and value of the components of the sales enablement program. Measures may include asset usage or downloads, asset impact on a sale as well as sales force rankings, and perceptions of enablement assets.

## Addressing Internal Issues With Best Practices

Many factors are involved in effectively equipping sales teams with the tools to help them have relevant conversations with customers. Agreeing to common enablement goals within the organization, having a strong understanding of customer needs and ensuring a closed loop approach is adopted are a few factors that can support an effective program. Additionally, key issues exist today that may prevent sales enablement from being effective.

- **Separate initiatives between marketing and sales**. Forrester Research calls these initiatives "random acts of sales enablement."[2] These random acts can create significant problems for the entire organization, from ineffective budget allocation due to duplication of efforts between departments to overwhelming the sales force with too many tools leading to very little getting used.

• **Sales-enablement tools that are not supported by a proper deployment program that increases awareness and provides education.** Effectively communicating the availability and intent of the tools is the first step in ensuring adoption. It is also imperative that some education or training on tool usage and tool intent is part of the program. The training should explain why the tools were created and how they should be used within the customer problem-solving cycle. Sales reps will not use a tool if they're not clear on its intent. Best practices can help address these issues.

## Best Practices for Sales Enablement

Through the creation of many sales-enablement programs from a variety of industries, a list of best practices was developed that can be applied to various stages of sales-enablement development, from planning through implementation. Three of these best practices are described in detail.

1. **Make sure the sales team has a seat at the planning table.** Sales people should be represented during the planning stage for all sales enablement initiatives since they will ultimately be the ones using what's produced. Their input at the initial stages can save significant time and money throughout the development process. At the onset of planning any enablement program, make sure goals between marketing and sales are aligned. Success depends on everyone moving toward the same goal.

Additionally, marketing must have a clear understanding of how sellers sell, what hurdles they must overcome and what tools work for them today. This further supports alignment between marketing and sales organizations. Interviews with various types of sellers can provide insight into what works today. An effective method for validating sales input is to shadow sales calls to witness their interaction with customers. This can uncover approaches to selling that aren't apparent through interviews.

*"Additionally, marketing must have a clear understanding of how sellers sell, what hurdles they must overcome and what tools work for them today."*

After getting input from sales for the planning stage, continue to engage the sales team throughout the process by including input milestones during development and implementation phases. This ensures buy-in prior to the formal release of any sales-enablement tools or support, and further supports alignment and provides a platform for joint ownership between marketing and sales. Finally, solicit input after the tools are published for ongoing refinement and improvements to sales programs.

> *"Simplicity comes from a concise, cohesive approach to sales enablement where information is provided in a centralized, consolidated manner."*

2. **The golden rule: It's all about simplicity.** Simplicity comes from a concise, cohesive approach to sales enablement where information is provided in a centralized, consolidated manner. To determine what gets produced, include a shared planning and prioritization approach between marketing and sales. This can be accomplished by monitoring what's being used by sales reps today and identifying what successfully drives a sale. By auditing what materials exist, what is currently being used, and what needs to be created to fill the gaps, companies can consolidate efforts and prioritize what's most valuable. Finally, simplifying how sales people locate and access the tools will help improve adoption and usage. A central hub, where critical sales-enablement tools reside, eliminates the need for sales reps to visit multiple locations to find what's available. This centralization increases the chance that the enablement tools will be found in the first place.

3. **One size does not fit all: varying skills and approaches require tiered enablement.** Sales people vary in their expertise and skill level. Different skill levels require different types of enablement. Some sales reps may be ready to sell more complex solutions; others may not.

> *"Different skill levels require different types of enablement."*

A sales-enablement program must provide tools for all levels to be successfully adopted across the entire organization. If budget limitations prevent enablement for multiple tiers, a prioritization exercise based on the greatest potential for return on investment should be applied.

# CASE STUDY
# CDW Sales-Enablement Program

Leopard Communications developed and launched an enablement program for a division of CDW. The three best practices previously described were leveraged and a program was designed to drive sales reps to focus more on solution sales in addition to transactional sales.

**The Client.** CDW is a national reseller of technology hardware, software and services.

**The Challenge.** CDW needed to remain a top technology products provider while selling more technology solutions and services. To do so, the sales team needed education and tools to sell the solutions. Additionally, marketing and sales identified an opportunity to partner. This had the potential to create a foundation for better collaboration, and the opportunity for sales to leverage customer-facing direct marketing activities as a "reason to call."

**The Journey.** In order to fully understand what was needed to expand the sales force capabilities from selling transactional products to complex solutions, a discovery phase was implemented to assess how the organization currently sold and supported sales. The discovery phase included interviews with different types of sellers, shadowing of select sellers, an audit of existing tools and platform usage, key stakeholder input and attendance at training sessions. Insights on seller behavior became the foundation for findings, recommendations and a comprehensive sales-enablement program plan. The plan included not only recommended prioritization of tool development, but also effective methods for communicating what enablement was available, how to use the tools, and a variety of metrics to measure adoption and usage.

**The Insights.** Key insights gleaned from the research drove overall findings and recommendations. These insights became the foundational structure of the sales-enablement program. The research showed.

- Providing too much sales support resulted in very little usage.
- When made aware of what marketing was sending to customers via direct marketing efforts, sales reps had additional opportunities to follow up with customers.
- A tiered sales force means not all sellers are ready to sell all solutions.

**The Solution.** Leopard Communications developed a comprehensive sales-enablement program that supported moving sales reps from awareness to adoption of the tools produced. The program included: a communications plan with a repeatable cadence to effectively inform sellers of tool availability; a centralized, simplified sales portal that served as the central hub for sales tools related to marketing efforts underway; a tiered approach for tool development to ensure there were tools created for those ready to sell solutions as well as those who were not; and, a prioritization of tools, including immediate and longer-term initiatives to fit within budget parameters. Additionally, external-facing marketing messages and internal sales tools were aligned, supporting an integrated message across customer touch points.

> *"Additionally, external-facing marketing messages and internal sales tools were aligned, supporting an integrated message across customer touch points."*

**The Implementation.** Leopard and the CDW client worked to identify core areas of content and key solution areas to be included on the new portal. An information architecture (IA), along with a creative look, was created to establish site sections and site navigation. The sales portal was piloted with select sellers. All modifications and refinements were done based on their input. Sales management training and support materials were provided to support management in explaining the intent of the portal. Lastly, a communications cadence announced the launch of the portal to the sales organization of the CDW division.

**The Results.** The enablement program and portal saw high adoption rates by sales within the first year with quarterly increases in visits, return visitors and new visitors. Page views, sales guide downloads and time-on-site also increased. In addition, there was an increased awareness of marketing campaigns going to customers, which provided an additional opportunity for the sales force to contact their customers. The sales-enablement approach continues to gain traction within CDW today, as it has grown from a pilot with one division to universal adoption by all divisions within CDW.

---

1. Forrester Research. *Sales Enablement Defined; Sales Enablement Is The Bridge Between Go-To-Market Strategy And Tactical Execution.* Scott Santucci. August 4, 2010, p. 15.

2. Forrester Research. *Sales Enablement Defined; Sales Enablement Is The Bridge Between Go-To-Market Strategy And Tactical Execution.* Scott Santucci. August 4, 2010, p. 13.

## CDW centalized sales portal, GETit

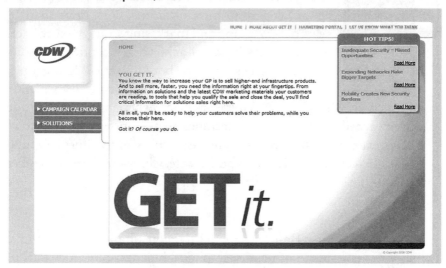

## CDW Sales Toolkit: Sales guides, calendar, solution diagrams

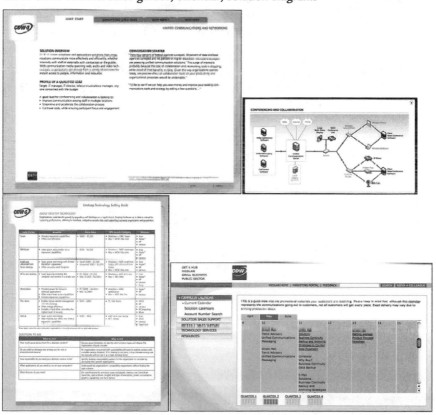

**Cheryl Ader Smith** is the executive director of strategy at Leopard Communications. With more than 18 years of advertising and marketing strategy experience, her focus has been on achieving exceptional results through sound strategy on both B2B and B2C accounts, including CDW, United Airlines, Ben & Jerry's, Blue Cross Blue Shield, and Winter Park. Her experience and aptitude have earned her positions at national creative powerhouses. Areas of specialty include technology; health, fitness and wellness; natural foods; travel and tourism; and health care. Cheryl has been a member of BMA Colorado since 2005.

**Lisa Haldeman**, executive consultant, brings a unique blend of relationship- and business-building skills to Leopard's client service team. Drawing on more than 19 years of agency experience, Lisa works closely with a team of strategy and account directors. Her close team collaboration puts her in the ideal position to act as a consultant when helping clients accelerate the sales cycle through brand stewardship, marketing and channel enablement. Lisa graduated from the University of Minnesota. She joined BMA Colorado in 2005.

# 20 | Inside Mirror Marketing Psychology

Melanie Hughes Goetz

**Y**ou might think advertising is nothing more than smoke and mirrors. And to some degree, you'd be right. Think of it this way: Marketing is a lot like magic. In either situation, what appears to be a mystery is actually a case of understanding how we humans process data.

At INVESCO Stadium at Mile High, Denver, Colorado, the fan "wave" is a football institution. Sitting in the thunderous, emotionally charged bleachers it evokes an instantaneous, physical reaction. As dedicated fans, we anticipate its arrival and never question the moment. As the wave arrives, we proudly throw up our hands and jump from our seat as if we had all practiced the tim-

> *"What appears to be a mystery is actually a case of understanding how we humans process data."*

ing. The wave often starts with just one person and yet has the power to set off a chain reaction of thousands. It builds slowly and, like a real wave, reaches its peak then crashes to a calm. What's interesting is how marketing can tap into this same human need to mimic each other — especially in groups. It is this same phenomenon of action and reaction on which mirror marketing is based. This is why businesses have been capitalizing on the predictability of this aspect of human nature for decades. In fact, this type of behavior takes place all the time, both in our personal and professional lives — whether we recognize it or not. It's that magical point where behavioral science shakes hands with advertising, resulting in profitable results for retailers as well as B2B companies. The only difference for B2B companies is in the methodology required.

## Background

The year was 1977 and it was the beginning of the end for traditional advertising. The Internet didn't exist, personal computers were in their infant stage, and electronic mail wasn't even on the horizon. Marketers had no fax machines, overnight air or cell phones. Communication was in person or by landline telephones. And written messages took days to receive. Today's instantaneous text-and-send technology — not to speak of an entire world of self-appointed journalists who blog everything and anything their hearts (and often times ill-informed minds) desire — has spawned a new business world. At the same time, it has created a whole new way for companies to utilize mirror marketing, with B2B being no exception.

Back in the early 1990s, neuroscientists Giacomo Rizzolatti, Vittorio Gallese and Leonardo Fogassi of the University of Parma in Italy, theorized that human actions are affected in the brain by mirror neurons. Continual research in this area by other academics continued to confirm the effects of triggering mirror neurons through sensory suggestion.[1] It has much to do with how people's brains are inherently wired and how people are driven to conform. The psychology behind mirror marketing helps explain the advertising missteps of some of the biggest companies, as well as provides a greater understanding of why other businesses flourish. A good analogy is the "monkey see, monkey do" approach. Just by knowing how people want to fit in or conform, your business can integrate its products into the lives of its customers. There is nothing more powerful to an advertising campaign than leveraging our basic human need to "mirror" each other.

## Mirror Marketing

Take for example, Udi's Handcrafted Foods.[2] Breaking into long-established American food suppliers' contracts and highly sought-after shelf space is no easy task. So how did an unknown guy from Israel get his food in the door of more than 10,000 food stores? Udi Baron combined his European bakery training with his native, cultural understanding of people. He is an entrepreneur with a natural talent for mirror marketing techniques.

Initially a wholesale operation, Udi's earliest accounts were corporate convenience stores located inside tall, Denver office buildings. He personally took his freshly baked breads and sandwiches to the administrative assistants and office managers, going floor-by-floor from top to bottom. The smell, the taste of newly integrated healthy sandwich ingredients coupled with the enthusiasm of its founder led to securing his first 1,000 accounts within two years of starting his business.

But breaking into major grocery suppliers, such as King Soopers (owned by the Kroger chain), Whole Foods, and Costco (nationally) required an extremely aggressive, mirroring approach. His phone calls were met with great resistance. Food buyers asked Udi to just send samples. He politely refused, insisting that his products must be created fresh and sampled in person. So, Udi found out when the Costco buyers were holding their weekly group meeting at their San Diego, California, facility and flew there personally.

With no formal appointment, Udi took a calculated risk. What he did know was the important mirroring opportunity of a group taste sampling. He believed the sensory reactions of each individual would feed onto the rest. Indeed it did. It facilitated a marketing B2B "push" (when a new product is introduced and demand is created from the top down) strategy resulting in a Costco "road show," which are weekend in-store promotions direct to consumers.

"Distributors and buyers are people just like anyone else and they are influenced in the same way to make decisions for their businesses of what their customers will choose to buy," says Udi. "Make no mistake, breaking into any established market takes more than timing and strategic business plans. It takes being able to show people why your product is better for them than what they already have." For Udi, an important niche was also developed through boutique, natural food stores such as Vitamin Cottage — where built-in consumers were searching for more organic offerings — making his all-natural granola products a perfect fit.

To underscore the impact of his implementation of mirroring, for the first fifteen years of operation Udi did not use traditional marketing or hire sales employees. He is only now lightly dabbling with a bit of social media where, since June 2010, the company had already amassed over 20,000 fans on Facebook. "We've never done typical branding," says Udi. "Our DNA is in having great products and in creating demand for them. For us, it is all about getting in front of the buyers that are the leaders in their industry."

Udi believes the success of any company is in developing customer loyalty that can withstand its competition. Clearly resourceful and motivated, he preferred to control risk by creating a distinct variety of packaged products. Handcrafted success has blossomed from a three-person family operation to hundreds of employees nationally manufacturing products for major food supply chains.

## The Methodology

While the methodology of applying mirror marketing in B2B situations may not appear to be as obvious when compared to the more practiced retail avenues, the reason it works is the same. In Udi's case, he implemented a form of mirroring called "social validation." The personal contact and explanation to potential buyers literally "validated" the product, substantiating its desire in the larger marketplace. That validation is essential.

Because B2B is often one-on-one, it's important to promote products in a way that motivates others to get in line. It means defining and conveying the group to the buyer, even if it is "virtual" rather than physical. Often this type of "grouping" is done through leveraging testimonials and industry standards. It works because people, in the case of B2B buyers, are naturally compelled to conform to the industry leaders, just as consumers are driven to fit in with their peers. Once he convinced Costco that his healthy products would create their own demand through sampling, other retailers soon followed suit.

# Mirror Marketing Pull

Mirror marketing strategies to stimulate B2B sales is not a new concept. One of the most notable examples of the "pull" (a consumer's desire for a product "pulls" it through the distribution channels from the bottom up) method of mirror marketing goes back to the mid-1980s. When sales orders for Ray-Ban sunglasses were dwindling from its retail distributors, the manufacturer decided to create consumer demand through a method of advertising which, at that time, was untested as to its effectiveness.

Enter actor Tom Cruise starring as a "Top Gun" Navy fighter pilot in what became the breakthrough movie of 1986. Throughout the film, Cruise flashed his signature smile while slowly removing his Ray-Ban aviator sunglasses. An instant attraction magnified on the big screen sold the image of the larger-than-life hot guy who got the hot girl. The "pull" of demand came from consumers asking retailers for the Ray-Ban sunglasses, which then drove the retailers to stock more inventory. You get the idea. Within weeks of the movie's premiere, sales of Ray-Ban's aviator sunglasses rose by over 40 percent![3] It was also noted that after the movie aired, Navy recruitment increased by a whopping 500 percent, which was an interesting side benefit for the Navy and our country.

Here's how it happened. The subconscious processing that takes place in our brains actually fires off a message that says "get the Ray-Ban aviator sunglasses and you'll look like that guy!" Sure, neuroscientists use words like "cognitive" and "insula effect," but the bottom line is, just like the "fan" wave at the stadium, it happens almost organically. When a popular celebrity looks cool because of a tangible product, like Tom Cruise in "Top Gun," any male over the age of puberty wants to duplicate — or mirror — the action and purchase that same pair of sunglasses to attain a similar outcome.[4]

Ray-Ban's ability to integrate the predictability of human nature into their sales efforts as product suppliers was instrumental to achieving impressive sales results. It worked so well they tried it again with "Men in Black" and the FBI-looking sunglasses. The strategy garnered the same results.

Another, somewhat stickier, example was initially born from a mistake. When 3M's Post-It Note was officially introduced in 1980, (thirteen years after the Post-It Note glue was accidently invented by 3M scientist Spencer Silver), it wasn't a huge success. Far from it. At that time, Post-It Notes were being promoted in offices only, but the businesses weren't buying. Having evolved from an unsuccessful attempt to be a tight-holding glue, the semi-holding glue of the Post-It Note was considered, at that time, to be a total bust in more ways than one. The product was going to be discontinued. However, the brand manager for the Post-It Note wasn't giving up. Not just yet. In a last ditch marketing effort, he mailed copious amounts of product samples to 499 CEOs of the Fortune 500 companies. (Note: 3M is a Fortune 500 company.)

The critical factor of the brand manager's effort was his ability to recognize how Fortune 500 CEOs are the equivalent of the "Tom Cruise strategy" to other business managers. Basically, what he did was brilliant. By recognizing that the CEOs of the Fortune 500 companies were indeed leaders in their respective industries, he established a group to be "mirrored" by others as well as each other. The sales of Post-It Notes rocketed. And as they say, the rest is history. Today there are at least 1,000 different forms of Post-It Notes being sold in 150 countries.[5]

According to author Jonah Lehrer of How We Decide: "Marketers have to realize that much of the decision-making process is carried out by the emotional parts of the brain. Reams of facts and figures won't compete with sensory appeals, stories, emotional pitches and other techniques that will be processed, not by the prefrontal cortex, but by more primitive parts of our brain — in most cases, the latter are the real 'deciders.'"[6]

## Integrating Mirror Marketing in B2B Efforts

The principles of integrating mirror marketing into your B2B marketing efforts are relatively simple. The first step is to create groups out of your buyers. Buyers don't need to be physically together to be considered a group. That's because people, even buyers, are always comparing themselves and their businesses to their peers and competitors. When people perceive they are out of sync with others, they will adapt or, in this case, mirror what others consider is the industry standard.[7]

The second step is to get buyers familiar with their group. This can be done with testimonials using video, or verbally through stories of others in their group. Sales and motivation consultant Cavett Robert said, "Since 95 percent of the people are imitators and only five percent initiators, people are persuaded more by the actions of others than by any proof we can offer."[8] It's important to understand that when your customers perceive your product is popular, that's enough to get them to purchase. They don't want to be left out. It can be as simple as displaying a tabulation counter on the website of the number of other businesses wanting your product.

The final step is to "socially validate" what you're selling to potential buyers. That means conveying that the "wave" of enthusiasm for your products is occurring for many reasons. Your product should be perceived as the industry norm and what successful business leaders find useful. Remember, the way your products are perceived can be more important than reality. Max Sutherland, marketing psychologist and business consultant, explained this phenomenon best: "The more a brand is advertised, the more popular and familiar it is perceived to be. We, as consumers, somehow infer that something is popular simply because it is advertised. When people are buying gifts for others, social proof is one of the most effective tactics that a sales clerk can use."[9] True, just by conveying the popularity of a product or service, this can create demand leading to a greater flow of sales.

## It Just Takes One

Think of the businesses you have purchasing your products or services similar to a series of dots. It starts with one. Just like Udi, once he got his first B2B sale, the rest started falling in place. When the behavioral dots are connected properly, you can achieve predictable sales results. Just like the mirroring that happens with the fan-crazed football "wave," it takes the initiators (the five percent) to validate and lead the charge for your B2B products or services. Find them. Connect with them. And most importantly — leverage them.

---

[1] Article/Research. "The mind's mirror." *American Psychological Association.* October 2005, Vol. 36, No. 9, pg 48

[2] Excerpt from a personal interview conducted by Esty Atlas, Hughes and Stuart, Udi Baron, owner/founder, Udi's Handcrafted Foods, Denver. September 21, 2010.

[3] Lindstrom, Martin. *Buy-ology: Truth and Lies About Why We Buy.* New York: Random House, 2008.

[4] Lindstrom, Martin. *Buy-ology: Truth and Lies About Why We Buy.* New York: Random House, 2008.

[5] Newman, Andrew Adam. *Turning 30, An Office Product Works At Home.* New York Times, July 27, 2010.

[6] Lehrer, Jonah. *How We Decide.* Houghton Mifflin Harcourt, 2009.

[7] Mortensen, Kurt W. *Maximum Influence: The 12 Universal Laws of Power Persuasion.* New York: AMACOM Books, American Management Association, 2004, page 72.

[8] Cavett Robert, *Personal Development Course.* Englewood Cliffs, New Jersey: Prentice Hall, 1966.

[9] Cody, M., J. Seiter, and Y. Montague-Miller. *Men and Women in the Marketplace: Gender Power and Communication in Human Relationships.* Hillsdale, New Jersey: Erlbaum, 1995, pp. 305-329.

References

Lakhani, Dave. *Subliminal Persuasion: Influence and Marketing Secrets They Don't Want You to Know.* Hoboken, New Jersey: John Wiley and Sons, 2008.

Lindstrom, Martin. *Brand Sense: Sensory Secrets Behind The Stuff We Buy.* New York. Free Press, Division of Simon and Schuster, Inc., 2005.

Mortensen, Kurt W. *Maximum Influence: The 12 Universal Laws of Power Persuasion.* New York: AMACOM Books, American Management Association, 2004.

Renvoise', Patrick, and Christopher Morin *Neuromarketing: Understanding the "Buy Buttons" in Your Customer's Brain.* Nashville, Tennessee: Thomas Nelson, Inc., 2002.

 **Melanie Hughes Goetz**, MBA, has been president of Hughes & Stuart Marketing in Denver since 1981. Her tactical marketing experience in public relations, brand messaging, crisis management, and the media serves her clients on many levels. Melanie brings a refreshing, very hands-on, down-to-earth style to sustainable marketing such as water and energy efficiency. She speaks on the benefits of opening the lines of communication, how to motivate the public, the cost-effectiveness of social vs. traditional media, and the importance of understanding basic human behavior. She co-authored *Roadrunner Marketing* and is a regular contributor to *Colorado Business Magazine*, online edition, as a marketing expert. Melanie joined BMA Colorado in 2010.

# MEASURING
# SUCCESS

ADVICE FROM THE TOP

# 20 | Driving ROI Into Today's Marketing Programs

## ROI 101: The Importance of Measuring Marketing Programs, Strategies and Tactics for Successful Execution

Byron O'Dell

I n today's environment, measuring the return on investment (ROI) on marketing programs is no longer a luxury. However, this does not need to be cause for alarm. A good marketing program can be a great marketing program when it appropriately considers how program elements will be measured. Adequate measurement is the key not only to understanding the payback for the company, but also to improving future programs.

> *"It is critical to know what is working – and more importantly, what is not working – before senior leadership does."*

## Measuring Marketing Programs

All good marketing professionals have programs which don't go as expected. They toil away on the messaging, offer, target audience, media schedule and all the other hotly debated elements. They spend the money but despite everyone's best efforts, the program fails. To some extent these less-than-perfect outcomes are expected. They serve as evidence the marketing professional is trying new tactics – something all marketing teams should be encouraged to do. In situations like this it is important to remember the words of the great hockey player, Wayne Gretzky: "You miss all the shots you never take." Successful metrics programs are about paying careful attention to what is working, and what is not, in order to improve future results.

There are several reasons a marketing professional should measure the ROI of his/her marketing program. These include:
- Improving program effectiveness
- Developing budget
- Demonstrating corporate responsibility

Clearly the most obvious reason to measure marketing programs is to improve the overall program effectiveness. In the words of advertising pioneer John Wanamaker, "Half the money I spend on advertising is wasted; the trouble is, I don't know which half." It is critical to know what is working — and more importantly what is not working — before senior leadership does. This gives one time to invest more heavily in lucrative tactics, launch countermeasures or simply stop those non-working tactics completely.

The second reason to measure marketing activity is to accelerate marketing funding. The last few years have been challenging for most marketing departments due to economic uncertainty. As organizations scramble to control costs, marketing budgets are often seen as long-term investments which must be sacrificed to cover short-term financial realities. Although accentuated lately, this is certainly not a new phenomenon. Most organizations ebb and flow these marketing budgets based on the overall health of the business. The root cause for this behavior is clear: Organizations often see marketing as a luxury which can be sacrificed and "restarted" with little risk to the business. In some cases this is true. However, an effective marketing-measurement program can demonstrate the real opportunity cost of such behavior, mitigate this continuing behavior and hopefully, reverse the marketing department's fortunes in the next downturn.

Notwithstanding the macroeconomic factors, there are practical reasons as well. Adopting the "ostrich" approach only yields lower budgets. Today in corporate board rooms, most new and sustaining marketing programs are measured against other growth-related investment options such as adding additional sales resources, upgrading information technology (IT) infrastructure, adding inventory, raising sales pay plans, etc. Not only must marketing always fight for its new programs, but it must demonstrate the fiscal responsibility of previous programs. The most effective way to do this is with information and results sliced in a way an executive finds relevant and compelling enough to support sustained and expanded marketing programs.

The third reason to measure marketing programs is to demonstrate corporate partnership and responsibility. As mentioned previously, all investments today are scrutinized to an unprecedented level. Marketing professionals must demonstrate they are a safe pair of hands to manage these precious marketing funds going forward. Although this seems obvious — after all, most functional departments have key performance indicators (KPIs) — simple enhancements to marketing programs can provide the confidence to ensure the funds are spent wisely. The special note here is that not all KPIs have to show every marketing dollar was executed perfectly or every program was a huge success. To a large extent, the marketing professional is expected to make mistakes by trying programs which are inherently risky. After all, good marketing is often about taking chances.

Senior leadership can often tolerate — at least for a short time — marketing misses as long as the marketing professional is conscious of the miss and is providing a roadmap to improve results. Where marketing professionals get in trouble is when an executive senses marketing failure without prior notification from the marketing team. Such behavior usually suggests the marketing department is out of touch with the business and usually results in senior leadership intervention. On a positive note, the more alignment the marketing metrics provide, the more runway the marketing team has to be aggressive in future marketing efforts.

Improving program effectiveness, developing the budget and demonstrating corporate responsibility are key reasons to measure marketing programs. But how do you implement a marketing metrics program?

## Tips And Tactics

In terms of a general marketing mindset, one must look for opportunities to implement metric systems to drive greater marketing visibility. Depending on the sophistication of the marketer's resources, whole categories of measurement are available. For example, deploying a customer relationship management (CRM) system such as Salesforce. com can provide a ready-to-go infrastructure. These CRM tools usually enable "lead to sale" tracking by campaign, vehicle, tactic and time. This assumes, of course, the commercial team will use this powerful interface to appropriately track and code the investments.

However, whether the marketer has a fully implemented CRM system or is building the initial pieces from scratch, a critical aspect of a reliable marketing program remains the ability to understand the difference between signal and noise. All sets of data, whether it is sales per day, leads per day, website visitors, click-through, etc. are subject to random variation. The key is to understand whether the data is trending in a significant direction versus just random chance. It is far too easy to look at data (marketing, sales or otherwise) and because one could "see" a positive trend, infer all efforts are

> *"Although not common training for marketing professionals, understanding statistics would allow most marketing professionals to improve their measurement fluency."*

working. Examine the same set of data under a statistical lens and it often becomes apparent the data set is inconclusive. More data are required to remove the causal factor of simple random chance. Today, marketers would be well served to understand common statistical analysis principles, such as normal distribution, standard deviation, confidence intervals and control charts. Although not common training for marketing professionals, understanding statistics would allow most marketing professionals to improve their measurement fluency. For the marketing professional looking to understand statistics in more detail, a good, quick read is *Understanding Variation* by Donald J. Wheeler.

Another great tactic to consider, from a general ROI standpoint, is new customer analysis. Customers leave for a variety of reasons — they go out of business, their business model changes, they are dissatisfied, etc. But new customers start buying for only one reason — they see value in the company's goods and services. As a marketing professional, seize the opportunity provided with all new customer signings. In large-scale customer databases, use e-mail techniques to interact with new accounts to determine what marketing tactics are effective.

In smaller customer databases, take the time to conduct a short interview. Start the conversation by thanking them for their recent business and, while on the phone, ask them about why they chose to buy. Were they persuaded by a promotional message? Do they even remember seeing a promotional message? Were they from a referral? Be diligent in gathering this information and sharing it in an actionable way with the marketing/sales organization. This is the most effective of all marketing feedback. Adding these customers to a tracking report can also be very effective. A revenue dashboard of new customers from marketing programs charting one-, two-, and three-year revenue would quickly demonstrate the value marketing is contributing to the business. Measuring significant changes in revenue from existing accounts can prove to be an effective metric as well — especially when these changes in behavior coincide with marketing programs.

The obvious corollary to the new customer metric is the lost customer metric. Where possible, conduct interviews with those accounts to determine what happened. As appropriate, those accounts can be added to the slow-drip or lead-nurturing program. Business changes are inevitable and both parties may be interested in renewing the relationship down the road. Staying in touch helps facilitate a future conversation.

## Campaign Guidance

Nearly all campaigns today have some element of digital marketing (online advertising, e-mail marketing, search engine marketing, etc.) The benefits to an online approach are very clear — rich media support, multiple offer testing, faster implementation, enhanced targeting and, for the benefit of this discussion, unprecedented traceability. If the marketing budget is tight, put a disproportionate amount of the budget in digital — traceable — vehicles. This way — win or lose — the marketing team has actionable feedback.

Every major promotional investment should include a measurement discussion. In the case of search engine marketing (SEM), one should always use campaign specific and keyword-specific landing pages. Far too many people do all the ground work to set up an SEM program — including competitive positioning, ad copy writing, keyword selection — only to, at the last minute, send all this expensive traffic to their homepage. It is critical to tie off the SEM keywords to a page that is relevant to the visitor and that strongly encourages the visitor to register or call. Without a strong call to action, the marketing professional is at real risk for unsatisfactory results. For print campaigns, deploy landing pages with vanity URLs to assist in traceability. Companies like www.tinyurl.com can make deep links easier to promote and track.

Use dedicated toll-free 800 numbers to assist in tracking wherever possible, print or online. Adding specific, or at a minimum campaign specific, 800 numbers is critical. In some industries, 50 percent or more of the responses to a promotional message are inbound calls. Without clear phone tracking, the marketing team can make false conclusions about campaign effectiveness. Operator training on the inbound phone call is also critical. Simple questions such as "How did you hear about us?" and "Which issue of magazine x are you looking at?" can go a long way in offering measurement clarity. Companies such as www.kall8.com make this process simple and affordable.

> *"Establishing a clear line of sight into marketing effectiveness makes it easier to create changes with confidence."*

Once marketing tracking is in place, share the results of the program's effectiveness with the extended marketing team — leadership, coworkers, consultants and agencies. Use this data to celebrate wins, admit defeats and adjust the approach. Design the next campaign to take advantage of the newly installed measurement tactics and to work around holes in the measurement system. For example, if measuring new customers was a barrier in the first system, have the customer redeem a code/coupon to make it more visible for the next round. If the plan suffered from a lack of visitor traffic measurement, commit to a new Web structure to address these gaps. Establishing a clear line of sight into marketing effectiveness makes it easier to create changes with confidence.

Be sure to share campaign effectiveness with the company's sales team. The sales team relies, at least in part, on the marketing team to provide information such as prospect qualification, sales leads, sales collateral and product training. Ask the sales team for feedback and testimonials to help build camaraderie. In building this rapport, it is important to remember the rule of thirds. One-third of the people will generally be supportive of marketing efforts to grow the business because these individuals are generally positive. One-third of the people will generally not be supportive of marketing efforts because these individuals have had a bad prior experience or are generally negative to new ideas. That leaves a third of the audience — this is the critical audience for the marketing people. This middle third is looking for a reason to either feel positive or negative. The battle is for the middle. This is the audience the marketing professional needs to quickly identify and engage.

Do not be scared of measuring marketing effectiveness. Simple tactics can be employed to measure each step in the process. Digital marketing has enabled all marketers to gather information quickly and easily.

Just remember to apply statistical principles to the data to determine if there is truly a signal. Finally, remember there is no crime in launching a marketing program which fails. The crime is not knowing if it worked and repeating past mistakes.

## CASE STUDY
## Product Sample Program

**The Challenge.** A global B2B manufacturer was doing well penetrating existing accounts but needed more new customers. Despite existing marketing programs, including trade shows, direct mail and print/online advertising, the number of high-quality leads was insufficient to sustain growth and achieve its revenue targets.

**The Journey.** In order to solve this problem, the manufacturer knew it had to examine all aspects of its marketing program and began conducting a marketing-effectiveness audit. The manufacturer began examining recent sales successes looking for common denominators and conducted interviews with customers, prospects and their internal sales/marketing teams. The manufacturer also launched external market research to understand the brand preferences and purchase behaviors of the target audience.

**The Discovery.** After collecting and analyzing the data a common theme of the research emerged. It became clear most customers who tried the manufacturer's product became a future customer. Based on this knowledge, the company launched an ambitious marketing program designed to induce trial among new customers in its core industrial target audience.

**The Solution.** The big offer for the campaign was that new qualified customers could receive up to $1,000 in free product to install and evaluate the manufacturer's superior quality first hand. Some disclaimers were installed in the campaign to limit the manufacturer's risk, namely the account had significant future business potential and the account had to be truly new business. Also given the amount of free product and promotional dollars being invested, it was important for the company to be able to track the effectiveness of each tactic in the campaign.

**The Implementation.** After careful planning, custom landing pages were launched for each campaign tactic and a new 800 number was created. Web page analytic coding was embedded on landing pages to measure referral statistics and a qualification script was deployed for the team manning the 800 number. The sales and customer service teams were also armed with a special account number to record any new sample orders. All customers placing the sample order were interviewed by the marketing team in order to understand how they heard about the promotion and determine future potential for business.

**The Results.** When the dust settled on the promotion, over 400 prospects requested a product sample; of those, 200 became qualified leads and were sent to the field. The field sales team authorized 60 actual product samples. From these, over $5 million in new potential was identified and over $1 million in new sales were booked as a direct result of the program. Based on the marketing metrics system, the company was able to track the most effective tactics in the campaign as electronic newsletter sponsorships, white paper offers and search engine marketing. Based on these results and the ability to track program payback, the company authorized the program to continue well past its intended life cycle. The marketing department used the findings from this program to improve future programs and, going forward, the company now has a new, improved attitude toward measureable marketing investments.

**Byron O'Dell** has more than 15 years marketing experience on both the agency and client side. He holds a bachelor's degree in advertising from the University of Illinois-Champaign and an MBA from Regis University in Denver, Colorado. Byron is currently the director of marketing, Americas for Norgren, a $1 billion engineering and manufacturing firm. He has been a member of BMA Colorado since 2007.

# 22 | Maximizing Return on Marketing Investment (ROMI)

Sandra Zoratti and Lee Gallagher

## ROMI: Why You Should Care

**M**arketers today are under extreme pressure to perform better and better over time, and to measure and prove that performance through the metric of return on marketing investment (ROMI). Increasingly, boards are demanding quarterly, and even monthly, updates on marketing performance and ROMI has become the key metric of success to the business. It is the one metric which translates the language of marketing into the language of business. While this metric is critical for marketers to maximize and measure, simultaneously, this requirement has come at an extremely challenging time.

## The Struggle

The Internet has changed everything. Irreversibly. New online marketing channels — e-mail, blogs, social media, etc. — are multiplying and are easy to utilize in mass communication ways that are "low cost" and immediate. As a result, an onslaught of mass-produced, "cookie cutter" messages are being sent by marketers which, in reality, are simply overwhelming the consumer. This growing quantity of messaging — some sources say each consumer is assaulted with 3,000 messages a day — together with the generic and irrelevant nature of the messaging is driving consumers to take action. Tune out, block, do-not call and anti-spam actions enable the consumer to quickly and effectively ignore the marketer's messages. Even more compelling is the fact that 46 percent of consumers stated that they would consider defecting from a brand which continued to send them irrelevant messaging.[1] This statistic should be an urgent wake-up call to marketers. The root cause of the problem? Irrelevance. More specifically, there is a lack of targeted relevancy and personalization in communications from marketers to consumers. The consumers are in control, they know it, and they vote with their dollars and attention to say "Know Me or No Me." Given this dilemma, the key challenge for marketers is how to get relevant — and get relevant fast — in order to retain their customers, grow revenue and ultimately maximize ROMI.

## The Answer: The Data Drivers

To be relevant in today's environment requires the use of data blended with the marketing creative process. Historically, data seemed scarce and difficult to capture and store. Today, data is abundant. Companies like IBM, Google and Microsoft are investing heavily in business intelligence techniques because the new bottleneck is finding the tools to analyze and leverage all that abundant data. These large companies are promoting strategies that capture, manage and leverage data. *The Economist* recalls that IBM believes business intelligence "will be a pillar of its growth . . . It has invested $12 billion in the past four years and is opening six analytics centers with 4,000 employees worldwide."[2] Moreover, Amazon, Google and Microsoft have made their massive computing infrastructure available to clients. These new platforms collect, store and process data and dramatically impact business processes — especially marketing. This data-driven trend not only helps enable more precise marketing, it helps measure the results and drive increases in ROMI.

Poor data integrity, siloed data and inaccurate data have been cited by 76 percent of senior marketers as the main reasons they are not leveraging data to realize the full revenue potential of their current customers.[3] In addition, only 46.5 percent of marketers say they have good quality insights into retention rates, customer profitability and lifetime value.[4] Data must be utilized for companies to better understand their customers' needs and potential, build relationships, and create a richer, more loyal customer base. Thus today, there is a new era of marketing. The use of data-based customer insights blended together with the marketing creative process is the new mantra.

## Data Meets Creative: Precision Marketing is Born

Precision marketing is the new data-driven marketing approach that enables marketers to send targeted, meaningful and engaging information to specific customers or prospects at the most appropriate time. Data analytics and insightful algorithms are used to determine the best fact-based strategy and messaging, the right messages to the right target customer segments and the best channels to deliver those messages. Precision marketing is the ultimate customer-centric approach to marketing. It is driven by data-based customer insights and metrics that clearly measure marketing effectiveness. A precision marketing approach will help you extract rich and actionable knowledge about your customers. Customer insights become deepened and you learn what customers care about, what motivates them and what causes them to disengage. In return, this information enables you to: create meaningful targets and personally relevant content; offer solutions to your customers' needs; help create long-term, mutually beneficial customer relationships; and maximize ROMI.

Precision marketing is all about building better relationships, thus driving bottom-line growth. The fundamental principle of precision marketing springs from a new reality: more relevance equals more revenue.

Precision marketing is founded on principles of collaboration, loyalty and relevance, and it works. It has been proven across industries, across applications, across channels and across geographies. Precision marketing principles were applied to Best Western, the world's largest hotel chain. The precision marketing testing for Best Western addressed business travelers from its upper tier/high value segments. By reengineering its loyalty statements to include dynamic, customized promotions based on historical customer data and behavioral patterns, Best Western was able to generate a 278 percent ROI and incremental 30 percent revenue relative to the static messaging statements.[5] And that's just one example.

## Getting Started

Precision marketing results are proven and compelling; however implementing a full-scale data-driven approach is not simple. Smart marketers take a modular approach to get started, expanding in a prescriptive fashion using an iterative learning process. The most important step is the first one. An effective and manageable way to start utilizing precision marketing techniques is to set up an in-market pilot around one campaign and one subset of customers, then measure results, learn, adjust and build from there. The *Five Steps to Better ROMI* provides a sequential approach to building and executing precision marketing in your business.

### Step 1. Identify your problem
Before launching a precision marketing campaign, it is important to ask a few critical questions. The process begins by first identifying what problem, or pain point, you are seeking to address. For example, are you trying to reactivate dormant customers or achieve a greater response rate to a particular promotion? In the Best Western case, the goal was to re-engage loyal customers, get them to more fully participate in a fall promotion and increase their engagement at Best Western properties.

### Step 2. Evaluate and leverage your data
By analyzing the data, you can establish a fact-based view of key customer segments so your targets are clearly and effectively defined. In the Best Western case, historical data were used to identify a group of 100,000 high-value customers. These customers were divided into statistically balanced parts: a 50,000 test group (to receive the dynamic messaging) and a 50,000 control group (to receive the static messaging).[6]

### Step 3. Create your target campaign
The next step is to synchronize campaigns and determine the best message for the customer segment and channel. For Best Western, the test group received a redesigned statement using "dynamic" content and offers based on data analytics; the control group received the traditional "static" loyalty statement.[7] The new statement included cleaner, clearer, personalized mes-

saging, a unique message about their loyalty status, and highly targeted and relevant promotional messaging on the statement page — all driven by data-based customer insights and a basic data modeling.

### Step 4. Test and measure

Once a test campaign is launched, the next step is to measure the results based on a wide range of criteria and, most importantly, on bottom-line measures. In less than eight weeks, Best Western enjoyed impressive results, including an uplift of 39 percent in number of stays and a 30 percent increase in revenue for test vs. control group with an astounding 500 percent increase in Best Western MasterCard applications.[8] Overall results: a 278 percent ROI based on the 30 percent revenue increases and a 40 percent savings in paper.[9] The measurable results of this campaign clearly show the power of data-driven techniques as well as the proof that precision marketing is indeed effective and compelling. Subsequent in-market data points — across industries, companies and geographies — consistently support these positive results.

### Step 5. Refine and repeat

After the initial test, it's time to refine and repeat the steps above to produce the same or improved results. You need to understand why the results turned out the way they did and then you can take the trial, expand it in a modular fashion across your marketing portfolio and optimize ROMI. Tangible, measurable increases in ROMI give you the tools needed to communicate marketing successes to the board room. In the case of Best Western, the behavioral data from the promotion were captured, analyzed and used to append and enhance the customer data file. Your precision and your results become better and better over time.

The following case studies further demonstrate the power of utilizing and leveraging data to drive targeted, relevant communications and increase ROMI.

## CASE STUDY
## The Telecommunications Industry

**The Challenge.** In a difficult economic time, a leading U.S. cable provider needed a way to realize revenue from dormant customers while also fortifying loyalty through cross-sell engagement from active customers.

**The Client.** This large telecommunications company, "Telco," provides phone, cable and Internet services to its customers.

**The Journey.** The Telco company sought to utilize its "must-read" monthly transactional statement to communicate promotional messaging to generate revenue.

**The Discovery.** CSG Systems worked to help the large Telco transition from a cost-based communications vehicle into a revenue-generating communications vehicle.[10] CSG Systems brought together a three-way partnership with the Telco, CSG and InfoPrint.

> *"The majority of the test group responded to the offer within two weeks of receiving the statements..."*

**The Solution.** Precision marketing was utilized to create a strategy and approach for increased revenue. Expertise on transactional document composition and design, together with data analytics on historical customer purchases, were utilized to devise a solution to help the Telco generate incremental revenue. They added color to the statement to enhance readability and guide the readers to an important message asking customers to sign up for complimentary digital services. A trial was set up between a monochrome control group and a color test group.

**The Implementation.** Utilizing a monochrome control group of 50,000 and a color test group of 50,000, statements were produced using variable print technology to create each test group statement with unique personal messaging in color.[11]

**The Results.** This implementation resulted in a 27 percent uptick in response rate for the test group vs. the control group.[12] In addition, the majority of the test group responded to the offer within two weeks of receiving the statements, while only two percent of the control group responded in the first two weeks.

## CASE STUDY
## The Hospitality Industry

**The Challenge.** A large hotel chain wanted help in reactivating dormant customers who had not done business with the brand for one year.

**The Client.** The hotel chain is one of the largest hospitality companies and has properties around the world.

**The Journey.** Loyalty programs were used to help keep customers engaged and staying at the hotel properties. However, there was a large base of customers who had not returned to stay at this large hotel chain and it was unclear which of these customers might be targeted for reactivation.

**The Discovery.** An algorithm was developed to help mine the "dead data of dormant clients" and identify those dormant customers with a high propensity to reengage with the brand.

**The Solution.** Using the data algorithm, a large group of high-propensity dormant customers was identified and an in-market campaign was created to help re-engage a segment of these customers.

**The Implementation.** Using customer data, a customized, highly targeted campaign was designed to help reengage a segment of these high-propensity dormant accounts. The results of that campaign vs. the active customer base was measured.

**The Results.** In less than eight weeks, this precision marketing implementation delivered an astounding ROI of 1090 percent.[13] Revenue results — extrapolated to one full calendar year — translated into $1 million in potential incremental revenue for this subset of high-propensity inactive accounts.

## CASE STUDY
## The Publishing Industry

**The Challenge.** *Graphic Arts Monthly* wanted to increase subscriber loyalty, improve advertising response rates and integrate online and offline customer experiences.

**The Client.** *Graphic Arts Monthly*, a trade publication and website, is part of the Reed Publishing family.

**The Journey.** As advertising dollars moved from offline publications to online publications, *Graphic Arts Monthly* wanted to generate incremental advertising response to help retain advertising dollars and drive subscriber loyalty rates.

**The Discovery.** User-generated preferences for content, together with personalized content covers and purls (personalized URLs) were identified as ways to drive more magazine engagement and response.

**The Solution.** Customer data were the foundation of this application. In this case, customer data were extremely sparse, so InfoPrint helped create a unique online survey for *Graphic Arts Monthly* subscribers and asked those subscribers about their content preferences. The survey data were then utilized to create unique magazine covers for every single issue, utilizing the exact topics requested by subscribers together with their personalized information and purls.

> *"And most surprisingly, an astonishing 90 percent stated a clear preference for print magazines over e-readers ..."*

**The Implementation.** In order to produce these unique personalized magazines, multiple covers had to be created with document composition specialists, unique customer data and variable headlines and graphics. Digital color technology was used to create almost 70,000 unique magazine covers.[14]

**The Results.** A post-publication survey showed exceptional results. Sixty-three percent of subscribers said they would go online for more information when the advertising was customized. Seventy-eight percent said they are more inclined to re-subscribe if content is tailored to personal preferences. And most surprisingly, an astonishing 90 percent stated a clear preference for print magazines over e-readers (iPad, Kindle, Nook) with only 24 percent intending to switch to e-readers over time.

These brief case studies are tangible proof points (and there are more) from real companies with real customers and statistically valid, measurable results. The bottom line: Data-driven precision marketing works to increase ROMI.

## Call to Action

Smart marketers know that existing marketing techniques are becoming ineffective and extinct in today's on-demand, data-driven world. Customer behavior dictates that the era of mass messaging is over. Today's consumer demands relevant, timely marketing messages and offers that are tailored around their history with the company. They want companies to support, not intrude. To personalize a greeting is simply not enough. Marketers must take the next step to embrace data and implement precision marketing techniques that leverage customer insights and deliver meaningful promotions and timely content to willing customers. Marketers who ignore this data-driven mantra risk extinction. Precision marketing is a proven way to increase ROMI and to quantify results with sound metrics. Thus the call to action to marketers is a serious and urgent one. And, more importantly, it's a feasible and proven one.

---

[1] CMO Council. *Why Relevance Drives Response and Relationship: Using the Power of Precision Marketing to Better Engage Customers.* CMO Council, 2009

[2] The Economist. (2010, February 25). *A Different Game.* Retrieved 2010, from The Economist: http://www.economist.com/specialreports/PrinterFriendly.cfm?story_id=15557465

[3] CMO Council. *Why Relevance Drives Response and Relationship: Using the Power of Precision Marketing to Better Engage Customers.* CMO Council, 2009.

[4] CMO Council. *Why Relevance Drives Response and Relationship: Using the Power of Precision Marketing to Better Engage Customers.* CMO Council, 2009.

[5] CMO Council. *Routes to Revenue.* CMO Council, 2008.

[6] CMO Council. *Routes to Revenue.* CMO Council, 2008.

[7] Haire, T. Best Western Melds Old and New. *Response.* March 2009.

[8] CMO Council. *Routes to Revenue.* CMO Council, 2008.

[9] CMO Council. *Routes to Revenue.* CMO Council, 2008.

[10] InfoPrint Solutions Company. (2009, March 10). *Leading Cable Provider Selects InfoPrint and SCG Systems to Enable Personalized, Targeted Communications.* Retrieved August 2010, from InfoPrint.com: http://infoprint.com/internet/wwsites.nsf/vwwebpublished/ai_pr031009_transpromo_csg_us

[11] InfoPrint Solutions Company. (2009, March 10). *Leading Cable Provider Selects InfoPrint and SCG Systems to Enable Personalized, Targeted Communications.* Retrieved August 2010, from InfoPrint.com: http://infoprint.com/internet/wwsites.nsf/vwwebpublished/ai_pr031009_transpromo_csg_us

[12] InfoPrint Solutions Company. (2009, March 10). *Leading Cable Provider Selects InfoPrint and SCG Systems to Enable Personalized, Targeted Communications.* Retrieved August 2010, from InfoPrint.com: http://infoprint.com/internet/wwsites.nsf/vwwebpublished/ai_pr031009_transpromo_csg_us

[13] InfoPrint Solutions Company. (2010, May). *InfoPrint Solutions Company Data Analytical Team Delivers Four Digit ROI.* Retrieved August 2010, from InfoPrint.com: http://infoprint.com/internet/comnelit.nsf/Files/ROI/$File/ROI.pdf

[14] Graphic Arts Monthly. Giving Readers What They Want. *Graphic Arts Monthly.* January 2010, pp. 55-56.

**Sandra Zoratti** is the vice president of global solutions marketing for InfoPrint Solutions Company, a Ricoh Company. She leads the overall solution strategy, marketing, sales, integrated portfolio development as well as data-analytics and multi-channel communications for the Precision Marketing Solution. Sandra is recognized as a thought leader in the area of precision marketing — a practice using data-driven insights to create highly targeted and relevant marketing approaches to drive improvements in revenue, response and ROI. She has been a member of BMA Colorado since 2007.

**Lee Gallagher** is currently the director of precision marketing & sales at InfoPrint Solutions Company, a Ricoh Company. Lee leverages his past 18 years with IBM to influence his marketing efforts at InfoPrint. At IBM, he won every sales award available, including the coveted Lou Gerstner Award. Lee's key to success is his drive to deliver relevant solutions and targeted, yet measured, marketing to his customers. Additionally, he blogs, conducts research and writes articles on how to deliver revenue through relevance by the implementation of the Precision Marketing Framework. His work has been discussed in the Wall Street Journal, PBS, Business Week, and MSNBC. Lee joined BMA Colorado in 2009.

# 23 | Proven Direct Marketing Demand Generation Techniques

David Ariss and Susan Fantle

M arketers have been using the discipline of direct marketing for more than 100 years. Unfortunately, that fact has caused many of today's marketers to see direct marketing as an out-of-date practice. The introduction of innovative technologies and new channels for interacting with prospects, however, has not changed human nature. Human nature is what maintains direct marketing's position as a powerful, effective marketing approach in any channel — online or off.

The key to successfully using direct marketing in B2B demand generation is adhering to the fundamentals or best practices that consistently produce programs that meet or exceed forecasted response rates.

> **Direct Marketing Defined**
> Advertising is designed to change image. Direct marketing is designed to change behavior.

Result-driven marketers use direct marketing to meet the following three objectives:

1. Produce a measurable response of qualified leads.
2. Test campaign elements to become more educated about what does and does not work with the target audience.
3. Work toward achieving an acceptable cost per qualified lead.

Well-executed B2B direct marketing campaigns follow five tested rules.

## 1. Run the Numbers

In direct marketing, the numbers form the basis for every direct marketing decision. Those numbers should be based on a company's predetermination of what percentage of gross revenue it is willing to pay to generate an inquiry as well as the average number of conversions it requires at each stage of the buy cycle. Here is an example of the calculations a marketer might complete to determine the company's acceptable cost per inquiry.

| | | |
|---|---|---|
| Average Sale Price | $ 250,000 | $ 50,000 |
| Acceptable Percentage of Marketing Cost Per Sale | 10% | 10% |
| Acceptable Marketing Cost Per Sale | $ 25,000 | $ 5,000 |
| Average Closing Ratio for Qualified Leads | 20% | 20% |
| Allowable Cost Per Sale for a Qualified Lead | $ 5,000 | $ 1,000 |
| Marketing Qualified Leads to Sales Qualified Lead | 20% | 20% |
| Allowable Cost Per Marketing Qualified Lead | $ 1,000 | $ 200 |
| Inquiry to Marketing Qualified Lead | 25% | 25% |
| Allowable Cost Per Inquiry | $ 250 | $ 50 |

Whether a specific B2B direct mail, e-mail or other direct marketing campaign has the ability to produce the desired numbers depends on the product, the industry, the market, the economic climate and many more factors. However, calculating these numbers should always be the foundation for all direct marketing strategies.

## 2. Test and Track

Testing — the target list and/or media, the offer, the packaging, or the creative — is the means by which one achieves the greatest advantage of direct marketing. Testing is designed to get direct, real market insight into which prospect list, offer, channel and creative approach generate the most profitable return at the lowest price.

Testing should be conducted first on lists, then on media and finally on offers. Only when the winning lists and offers have been identified should creative directions be tested. Testing should be conducted in A/B splits to ensure accurate results and overcome seasonal and economic variations. An A/B split test is directly testing one campaign element to one part of the target market against another campaign element to another part of the target market during the same period.

### Minimum Numbers for a Valid Test

To be able to forecast a similar response rate on future marketing using results from past tests requires that the results be statistically valid. Statistical validity is determined by using accepted confidence tables (available from many direct marketing vendors). The general rule of thumb for a statistically valid response rate is that the number of individuals responding within a test cell must be greater than 105. This response provides an 80 percent level of confidence in the results within that cell

(50 percent rate or 50/50 is just random). If the results are less than 105 in any one test cell or test cell total, then the results cannot accurately predict the outcome of future campaigns using that combination of list and offer. Here is an example of a direct marketing test grid.

| | Prospect List #1 CIO Magazine | Prospect List #2 InfoWeek | Prospect List #3 Info U.S.A. | TOTAL |
|---|---|---|---|---|
| Free White Paper Offer | 10,000 | 10,000 | 10,000 | 30,000 |
| Free Demo Offer | 10,000 | 10,000 | 10,000 | 30,000 |
| Industry Trend Survey | 10,000 | 10,000 | 10,000 | 30,000 |
| TOTAL | 30,000 | 30,000 | 30,000 | 90,000 |

Many B2B marketers may look at this and say: "But my entire prospect universe is only 10,000 companies. If I were to test, none of the results would be statistically valid. So why should I bother to test?"

The key is not the number of prospects in each test cell but the percentage of response. A business with a smaller marketing universe can still achieve statistically valid numbers by either finding ways to achieve higher response rates or combining the results from repeated but identical campaigns.

## Common Direct Sales Tracking Tools

The ability to accurately track the results is one of the most important elements in testing. Many well-intentioned companies have failed in their testing efforts because of the inability to accurately track campaigns.

Responses to e-mail marketing are fairly easy to track. In direct mail or other offline channels, tracking is helped by the following approaches:

- The use of personalized URLs (PURLs) or a priority code to be entered when prospects respond online
- Different 800 numbers or extension numbers for each test cell
- A key code printed with the addressing info on a mail-back reply device

## Indirect Sales Channel Tracking Tools

Original equipment manufacturers (OEMs) who sell through distributors and resellers have a more difficult time tracking sales. However, here are a few tactics that are useful to ensure accurate lead tracking:

- **Online.** When prospect information is entered on landing pages, the data can be captured for record-keeping, then easily forwarded to the appropriate vendor.
- **Phone calls.** There are services available to receive prospect calls at the OEM level, where a live operator captures the tracking information, then instantly forwards the call to the appropriate sales outlet.
- **Direct mail reply cards.** The return address can be the OEM. Then the lead data can be entered and quickly distributed to resellers electronically.

## 3. Target the Right Prospects

Targeting can mean choosing the right mailing or e-mail list of prospects or customers. The placement of display advertising on selected vertical websites isn't a list; however, the same general approach is taken for selecting which sites to use for search engine marketing (SEM) as for selecting e-mail or direct mail prospect lists.

B2B mailing and e-mailing lists are more limited than consumer lists but generally fall into these categories:

- **Compiled:** built from public records, phone listings, etc.
- **Controlled circulation business publications:** online and offline subscribers to vertical business magazines that are provided free but require recipients to complete a questionnaire in order to receive
- **Paid circulation business publications:** online and offline paid subscribers to business publications
- **Association member:** membership lists to industry associations
- **Opt-in:** individuals who have opted to receive online newsletters, reports and other vertical industry information that is not available offline. These are subscribers who have also agreed to receive product information from qualified companies

## Evaluating List Quality

The important elements in judging the right B2B lists or media placements include the following:

- How were the records built? In the case of a website, who does the site attract and how many visitors does it have?
- Which other marketers have used the list or site multiple times (an indication that the site is successful for specific verticals)?
- If the list is mail or e-mail, how are the individual records updated?

- · How often are the records updated?
- · When were they updated last?
- · What selects are available on each record? (SIC code, title, # of employees, annual sales, branch vs. headquarters, geography, purchase-related data, etc.)
- · Is the list rental for one-time use, one-year use, or unlimited? (The better quality lists are for one-time use only.)
- · What is the minimum order?
- · How long after the list is ordered can it be delivered?
- What banner space is available, when and at what cost?
- What is the cost of the basic list? What is the cost for each select chosen? (These will vary.) Are there any additional charges?

During the list or placement research process, counts are obtained as to how many names fall into the desired target group for each list and within the desired geography. Testing multiple lists and sites is the best way to begin the testing process in direct marketing.

## 4. Make Effective Offers

In B2B demand generation, the goal is to get prospects to raise their hands — by asking for the information being offered — and show they are interested in the subject of the information and possibly the solution that would ultimately be offered. These offers — often called content — include such items as white papers, how-to booklets, checklists, webinars, demos and other content related to the business category.

## 5. Follow Proven Rules of Creative

The best messaging approach in demand generation is to sell the content or other offer and not the product or service. Although selling the product attracts responses from individuals who are already in the evaluation stage of the buying process, it misses the individuals who are just discovering they have a problem and are in the interest stage of the buying cycle.

## Focusing the Message

Whether the purpose of the campaign is to generate leads or make sales, the basic tenet of successful direct marketing messaging is to make sure it answers the prospect's question: "What's in it for me?"

Copy should focus on the benefits of requesting the content being offered. It should cover how the white paper, webinar, or report helps the prospect become more informed about how to solve the pain or problem they are experiencing. It should always include a clear, prominent call to action: download now, register now, sign up now, call now, etc.

## Supporting the Brand

Design has two major purposes. One is to make the messaging easy and inviting to read and the other is to support the brand. Showing a thumbnail visual of the item being offered makes it appear to be real and enhances the strength of the offer.

## CASE STUDY
## B2B Publisher Conducts Successful Direct Marketing Test

**The Client.** The real beauty of direct marketing for demand generation is its focus on testing multiple approaches to let the market show the most productive approach. A perfect example of this is a campaign conducted for a large national B2B technology publishing firm on the East Coast. Customers for this publisher are primarily marketing decision makers in technology companies seeking to reach their potential buyers.

**The Challenge.** In spite of previous marketing approaches used, the sales force of this publisher was unhappy with the volume of leads in the pipeline and was demanding that more leads be generated as fast as possible. This B2B technology publisher was looking for ways to generate more leads that could be converted to online advertisers, offline advertisers, and sponsors of the publisher's other informational services.

**The Discovery.** One of the publisher's newest sales leaders was familiar with the successful direct marketing approach to lead generation and suggested it to the marketing team as a powerful way to generate many leads quickly. The marketing team liked what they heard and followed the sales leader's recommendation to hire Ariss Marketing. Ariss Marketing was recommended because it had successfully implemented this campaign approach for other B2B marketers.

**The Solution.** Everyone likes to be asked his opinion — even six-figure executives. Everyone also likes an opportunity to see how their decisions and processes stack up against those of their peers. Using a trend survey to leverage these human traits is an excellent way to engage cold prospects — promising prospects who, if they participate in the survey, have an opportunity to see the results. This provides a strong incentive to respond.

The leads generated from a survey are soft leads. They do not represent individuals who have requested information to help them solve a specific marketing problem. For this reason, to test the performance of the above approach and generate more qualified leads, it was decided to test the survey directly against an offer for an informational white paper.

**The Implementation.** Primarily using its in-house list, augmented with highly targeted outside lists, 100,000 pieces were mailed to marketing titles in technology companies. Half of the pieces contained an invitation to prospects to participate in an industry survey. The invitation directed the recipient to complete the printed survey and mail it back or visit a PURL (personalized URL) to complete the survey online. The first 200 participants received an Amazon.com gift certificate for their participation.

In an A/B split test, the second half was sent the invitation to download the informational white paper. In addition, 15,000 survey invitations and 15,000 white paper offers were sent via e-mail to additional prospects. No recipient received both the direct mail and the e-mail.

**The Results.** The postal mail pulled 3.1 percent (3,100 leads) and the e-mail pulled less than 0.25 percent (75 leads). As predicted, the responses requesting the white paper were better qualified leads, but the survey and Amazon Gift Certificate offer generated a greater number of leads.

An interesting side note: of the 3,100 responses from the postal mail, 800 sent the paper survey in the supplied reply envelope rather than filling out the survey online — even though they still had to provide their e-mail address to receive their free gift. It had been assumed, because the audience was very IT oriented, that all of the responses would come in online. Giving prospects multiple ways to respond significantly lifted response.

Because of their lower campaign costs, many say e-mail campaigns are more cost-effective than direct mail, but this test proved otherwise — as have many similar tests conducted in the B2B marketplace. Yet the final determination in the effectiveness of any campaign is cost per sale.

## Conclusion

In this marketing era, with its strong focus on social media, the direct marketing approach is still a powerful tool in demand generation and lead nurturing. More than any other marketing method, it helps marketers forecast and control the number of leads that are generated from each campaign.

**David Ariss**, founder and president of Ariss Marketing Group, Inc. has been active in the direct marketing industry for over 25 years. After beginning his career in magazine publishing, he started his first agency in 1995. In 2002, and again in 2008, Ariss was awarded the prestigious Grand Eagle Award for Direct Marketer of the Year by the Rocky Mountain Direct Marketing Association. David is a very active volunteer for civic organizations and has been a guest lecturer on marketing at Johnson & Wales University. He became a member of BMA Colorado in 2010.

**Susan Fantle** owns The Copy Works. She has over 22 years helping companies produce high quality, productive direct marketing. She began her career as a copywriter in a traditional advertising agency and then spent eight years in direct sales. Today, her consulting focus is B2B and technology marketing. She is the recipient of two Gold Echo Awards as well as many other industry awards.

# 24 Using Voice of the Customer (VOC) to Measure Event Success

Barry Seidenstat

**M**arketing organizations are under increasing pressure to measure the outcomes of their investments. Organizations need data to determine their best marketing investments, be they print, social, Web or other marketing tools. This chapter demonstrates how to produce high-return event marketing that addresses the needs of attendees while delivering powerful, measurable, strategic results for your organization. Not only will you learn how to employ proven tools and evaluate attendee satisfaction, you will understand how the event affects what attendees think, feel, say and do during or after the event. And, more importantly, you will learn how to use this information to calculate your event's return on investment (ROI).

The process for developing measurable events need not be difficult or complex if you follow the following five-step process. Throughout the chapter, keep in mind that the Voice of the Customer (VOC) drives the measurement, the execution and the ROI. An important part of the process is to begin with the end in mind. Here are the ROI measurement process steps:

- The value of your event is determined by how well it achieves each of its objectives.
- Breakeven is where total cost equals total value created.
- Positive ROI is in proportion to the amount by which achievement of each objective exceeds the break-even level.

- The formula for %ROI is as follows:

    *%ROI = ((actual sum of objectives performance/sum of objective breakeven performances) x weighting) – 1*

In other words, the ratio of how well you achieved your measurable objectives is divided by the breakeven of those measurable objectives.

# Five Steps for Event ROI

### Step 1. Gathering Voice of the Customer data

Voice of the Customer is a qualitative and quantitative research technique that produces a detailed set of customer wants and needs organized into a hierarchical structure and then prioritized in terms of relative importance with current alternatives. Gather VOC by asking your audience, participants and stakeholders questions regarding what they need to drive business, be an advocate, increase investment, learn, etc. Review the outlined list of sample questions. These questions are similar to those used for sales or reseller or franchise audience.

## Sample Qualitative Questions

- What do you think are "Company Name'" strengths/weaknesses in the marketplace? Why?
- What do you think are "Company Name'" internal strengths/weaknesses at this time? Why?
- How confident are you that your "Company Name" business will be better next year than this year? Why do you feel this way?
- What do you think "Company Name" should do to improve: (Marketplace or internal weaknesses identified above)?
- What do you think "Company Name" leadership can do to specifically help you in improving your business?
- Looking towards the "Event," what objectives do you think the "Event" should achieve?
- What major concerns and issues do you have that you would like addressed at the "Event"?
- In your opinion, what does the "Event" have to accomplish for you to judge it a success?

The output of this research is the input to the development of your measurable objectives. Regardless if the research is quantitative or qualitative, it's important at this stage to make sure your results are credible, reliable, precise, accurate and actionable. It's also important to make sure you have buy-in from your event stakeholders. You'll need to perform stakeholder analysis to assess the attitudes of the stakeholders regarding potential event objectives. It's important to note that your stakeholders can be anyone in your organization who may be affected by the event's outcomes. Stakeholder analysis has the goal of developing cooperation between the stakeholder and the event project team and, ultimately, assuring successful outcomes for the project by assuring event objectives can be agreed upon.

Different types of events will naturally have different types of objectives. The Typical Event Objectives Chart is a list of different event types, typical objectives and their weights. The user conference is highlighted as an example to demonstrate the process for measurement against objectives. Objectives must be defined in terms of your business value, be measurable, and have weights assigned based on the importance to your organization and the potential to create organizational value.

## Typical Event Objectives

| Event Type | Typical Objectives (weights) |
|---|---|
| User/Customer Conference | Enhance brand perception (25%)<br>Promote purchase/upgrade (25%)<br>Increase customer loyalty (30%)<br>Understand customer needs (10%)<br>Grow event next year (10%) |
| Channel Partner Conference (dealers, resellers, franchisees) | Promote channel investment (45%)<br>Increase channel effectiveness at selling company products (25%)<br>Increase channel loyalty (15%)<br>Understand partner needs (15%) |
| Sales meeting | Training (50%)<br>Motivation (40%)<br>Increase employee loyalty/reduce turn-over (10%) |
| Executive team meeting | Team building (30%)<br>Information sharing (40%)<br>Decision making/business planning (20%)<br>Increase employee loyalty/reduce churn (10%) |
| Trade show (organizer) | Generate profits (70%)<br>Grow future events (30%) |
| Trade show (sponsor) | Generate qualified leads ((60%)<br>Enhance brand position (40%) |

- Define objectives in terms of business value
- Must be measurable
- Assign weights based on importance (potential to create value)

## Step 2. Defining quantifiable metrics

To define quantifiable metrics, you'll need to answer the question, "As measured by how?" Bear in mind, your measurement "how" must reliably measure the ultimate results. You'll generally suggest measurements that are based on how the event affects attendees: intentions, perceptions, preferences, attitudes, abilities and behaviors. In other words, what and how attendees think, feel, do and say after the event. We'll group these indices into a category called The Core Values (TCV) and reference them later.

The Directness vs. Ease of Measurement chart shows three important facts:

1. How and where the various data types will be measured.
2. The link between the metric and value.
3. The ease of collecting the data.

There are direct links between metric, value and ease of measurement. The more direct the measurement and the greater the value of the measurement, the more difficult it is to measure.

## Directness vs. Ease of Measurement

| | On-site Activities | TCV | Ultimate Results — Data |
|---|---|---|---|
| **Data Types** | Attendance, interactions, contact exchange | Survey responses | Varied: Sales, customer turn-over, employee retention, sales team performance, event profitability, event growth, etc. |
| **Ask...** | What observable behaviors will contribute to achievement of the objective? | How will TCV be different after the event if the objective is met? | How does achieving the objective affect the bottom line? |
| **Link Between Metric & Value** | Indirect<br>Requires inference to assess value | Moderate<br>Some inference required | Direct<br>Measures value driver itself |
| **Ease of Measurement** | Tool available | Survey and attendee participation | Can be challenging; Results from multiple inputs |
| | Easy | | Hard |

Next, you need to define possible metrics that you'll measure and the weight to be assigned to each one. The examples shown are suggested possibilities. Your organization may be different. The User/Customer Conference example, shown earlier, shows sample metrics and weight. The metrics are the most valuable for our sample organization.

## Define Possible *Metrics* and *Weight*
### (User/Customer Conference example)

Areas of Measurement

| | Event Objectives | On-site Activities | TCV | Ultimate Results |
|---|---|---|---|---|
| **Enhance Brand Perception (25%)** | | Attendance at key sessions<br>Comments re: TV spots<br>Attendance at Brand showcase | *Immediate improvement in brand perception (100%)* | Long-term improvement in brand perception |
| **Promote Purchase (25%)** | | *Qualified leads captured (60%)*<br>Attendance at key sessions, events<br>Prospect interactions w/ reference customers | *Improvement in intent-to-increase investment score (40%)* | Increase in sales |
| **Increase Customer Loyalty (30%)** | | Attendance at key sessions, events<br>1-1 meetings completed | *Improvement in customer satisfaction score (100%)* | Reduced customer turn-over |
| **Understand Customer Needs (10%)** | | *Product intro responses (50%)*<br>*Follow-up information requested from PM (50%)* | | Improved product development performance |
| **Grow Event (10%)** | | | Intent-to-return score | *Year-over-year growth (100%)* |

## Step 3. Determining breakeven for each metric

At this point, the actual planning of the event must take into account the event objectives. Event budget dollars and most importantly, event content should be strongly focused on delivering against objectives. Event content that doesn't drive towards delivering against objectives should be reduced or eliminated. If your attendees have told you the happy faces video at the end means nothing to them, don't spend money on it. Save it or invest it where it will mean something to the attendees. Obviously, you want your event to have a positive ROI. If you didn't, why would you be having it?

From the ROI equation shown earlier, you know you need to understand the net-total event cost including opportunity cost of employee time. For each metric, ask what the lowest performance level is that would make the event just worth holding, given the cost. Narrow in on your break-even level. Pick an achievable middle value. Determining the break-even level is a cross-functional exercise! Your key stakeholders must have input. They are the consumers of the results. What's important to sales may not be important to marketing. The next chart shows the previously developed sample objectives and metrics and the newly cross-functionally determined break-even level expressed in units to be measured. Notice that some measurement units are expressed as percentages, such as percent improvement or percent increase. Other measurement units are an actual numeric unit measure, such as number of interactions, responses or leads. The chart also notes the sample event cost of $1,400,000. That's a lot of money invested so you want to be certain the measurement metrics are correct.

### Sample Break-Even Performance Levels

| Event Objective & Weight | Metric Weight (MW) | Break-Even Level (Unit) |
|---|---|---|
| Enhance Brand Perception (25%) | Immediate improvement in brand perception (100%) | 10% increase in brand perception score |
| Promote Purchase (25%) | Qualified leads captured (60%) | 100 Qualified leads captured |
| | Improvement in intent-to-increase investment score (40%) | 10% increase Intent-to-increase investment score |
| Increase Customer Loyalty (30%) | Improvement in customer satisfaction score (100%) | 10% improvement in customer satisfaction score |
| Understand Customer Needs (10%) | Product intro responses on-site (50%) | 80 positive responses to roadmap |
| | Follow-up information requested from PM (50%) | 40 on-site interactions w/ PMs |
| Grow Event (10%) | Year-over-year growth (100%) | 5% year-over-year growth |

### Net Event Cost = $1,400,000

## Step 4. Gather tools and collect data before, during and after the event

The tools used to collect data depend on the data you are collecting. The event plan guides the measurable objectives tool-set. Your pre-event VOC provided qualitative and/or quantitative data to baseline your measurements or assist with setting your objectives. Post-event VOC, by way of surveys or self-serve kiosks, provides additional data measurements. You'll need to measure interactions, attendees and other live in-person activities. Look at the number and types of leads collected. And finally, review the total event spend, including overhead costs.

| Data Area | Tools |
|---|---|
| Event Plan | Budget, Defined & Measurable Objectives |
| VOC | Pre/Post Event: Interviews, Web survey<br>During Event: Pulse interviews, kiosk, personal smart device |
| Attendance | Door monitors, Radio Frequency Identification (RFID), business card, personal contact, etc. |
| Interactions | Card readers, notes, etc. |
| Leads | Closed-loop lead capture system |
| Cost | Spend analysis |

As a reminder, some tools and data collection may be more difficult than others. Do not be discouraged by this. Make sure you can use the tools and collect the data that supports the objective measurement requirements. As long as stakeholders are in agreement with both the objectives to be measured and the relevance and accuracy of the data collected, your results will be valid.

## Step 5. Run the calculations using the template provided

Now that your event is complete and you've collected the data, it's time to see how you did using the methodology in the chart provided. This gives you a quick and easy way to enter the data and make the calculations. First, insert the objectives and objective weight (OW) as described earlier.

## Calculation Template Step #1

Next, insert the metrics that were developed and the agreed upon suggested metric weight (MW) as described earlier. Multiply objective weight (OW) times metric weight (MW) to arrive at overall metric weight (OMW).

## Calculation Template
Step 1: Insert the Objectives & Objective Weight (OW)

| Event Objective | Objective Weight (OW) | | | | | | |
|---|---|---|---|---|---|---|---|
| Enhance Brand Perception | 25% | | | | | | |
| Promote Purchase | 25% | | | | | | |
| Increase Customer Loyalty | 30% | | | | | | |
| Understand Customer Needs | 10% | | | | | | |
| Grow Event | 10% | | | | | | |

## Calculation Template Step #2

Once you have your objective weight, insert your break-even levels (BE) as determined by your cross-functional team of event customers. Be sure to note the unit, such as percent (%) or number (#).

## Calculation Template
### Step 2: Insert Metrics & Metric Weight (MW) & Perform (OW)(MW) = Overall Metric Weight (OMW)

| Event Objective | Objective Weight (OW) | Metric | Metric Weight for Objective (MW) | Overall Metric Weight (OMW) | | | |
|---|---|---|---|---|---|---|---|
| Enhance Brand Perception | 25% | Immediate improvement in brand perception (%) | 100% | 25% | | | |
| Promote Purchase | 25% | Qualified leads captured (#) | 60% | 15% | | | |
| | | Improvement in intent-to-increase investment score (%) | 40% | 10% | | | |
| Increase Customer Loyalty | 30% | Improvement in customer satisfaction score (%) | 100% | 30% | | | |
| Understand Customer Needs | 10% | Product intro responses on-site (#) | 50% | 5% | | | |
| | | Follow-up information requested from PM (#) | 50% | 5% | | | |
| Grow Event | 10% | Year-over-year growth (%) | 100% | 10% | | | |

## Calculation Template Step #3

Insert your actual scores as measured before, during or after the event using the measurement tools noted earlier in step #2.

### Calculation Template
#### Step 3: Insert Break-even (BE) requirement score

| Event Objective | Objective Weight (OW) | Metric | Metric Weight for Objective (MW) | Overall Metric Weight (OMW) | Break-Even (Unit) (BE) | Actual Score | Actual vs. Break-even (ABE) (BE) / (AS) | Weighted Actual vs. Break-even (WABE) (ABE) (OMW) |
|---|---|---|---|---|---|---|---|---|
| Enhance Brand Perception | 25% | Immediate improvement in brand perception (%) | 100% | 25% | 10% | | | |
| Promote Purchase | 25% | Qualified leads captured (#) | 60% | 15% | 100 | | | |
| | | Improvement in intent-to-increase investment score (%) | 40% | 10% | 10% | | | |
| Increase Customer Loyalty | 30% | Improvement in customer satisfaction score (%) | 100% | 30% | 10% | | | |
| Understand Customer Needs | 10% | Product intro responses on-site (#) | 50% | 5% | 80 | | | |
| | | Follow-up information requested from PM (#) | 50% | 5% | 40 | | | |
| Grow Event | 10% | Year-over-year growth (%) | 100% | 10% | 5% | | | |

## Calculation Template Step #4

Now that all of our known data is entered, it's just a simple matter of running the calculations.

### Calculation Template
#### Step 4: Insert "As Measured" Achievement score

| Event Objective | Objective Weight (OW) | Metric | Metric Weight for Objective (MW) | Overall Metric Weight (OMW) | Break-Even (Unit) (BE) | Actual Score | Actual vs. Break-even (ABE) (BE) / (AS) | Weighted Actual vs. Break-even (WABE) (ABE) (OMW) |
|---|---|---|---|---|---|---|---|---|
| Enhance Brand Perception | 25% | Immediate improvement in brand perception (%) | 100% | 25% | 10% | 12% | | |
| Promote Purchase | 25% | Qualified leads captured (#) | 60% | 15% | 100 | 150 | | |
| | | Improvement in intent-to-increase investment score (%) | 40% | 10% | 10% | 15% | | |
| Increase Customer Loyalty | 30% | Improvement in customer satisfaction score (%) | 100% | 30% | 10% | 10% | | |
| Understand Customer Needs | 10% | Product intro responses on-site (#) | 50% | 5% | 80 | 100 | | |
| | | Follow-up information requested from PM (#) | 50% | 5% | 40 | 70 | | |
| Grow Event | 10% | Year-over-year growth (%) | 100% | 10% | 5% | 4% | | |

## Calculation Template Step #5

- First, determine % actual vs. break-even (ABE) by dividing (break-even level (BE)) by (actual score (AS)).

- Next, multiply (% actual vs. break-even (ABE)) x (overall metric weight (OMW)) to get (weighted actual vs. break-even % (WABE)).

- Finally, add up the percentages in the weighted actual vs. break-even (WABE) column. The total is the percentage above or below your actual performance over the break-even performance. A successful event will have a number greater than 100 percent.

- Now we can determine our event ROI using our formula: %ROI = ((actual sum of objectives performance/sum of objective break-even performances) x weighting) – 1

**(%) ROI = 121% – 1 = 21%**

**($) ROI = $1,400,000 x 21% = $294,000**

**This event returned a 21 percent ROI or $294,000 based on event value.**

### Calculation Template
**Step 5: Calculate as shown (BE/AS)(OMW)Sum (WABE) to get %ROI**

| Event Objective | Objective Weight (OW) | Metric | Metric Weight for Objective (MW) | Overall Metric Weight (OMW) | Break-Even (Unit) (BE) | Actual Score | Actual vs. Break-even (ABE) (BE) / (AS) | Weighted Actual vs. Break-even (WABE) (ABE) (OMW) |
|---|---|---|---|---|---|---|---|---|
| Enhance Brand Perception | 25% | Immediate improvement in brand perception (%) | 100% | 25% | 10% | 12% | 120% | 30% |
| Promote Purchase | 25% | Qualified leads captured (#) | 60% | 15% | 100 | 150 | 150% | 23% |
| | | Improvement in intent-to-increase investment score (%) | 40% | 10% | 10% | 15% | 150% | 15% |
| Increase Customer Loyalty | 30% | Improvement in customer satisfaction score (%) | 100% | 30% | 10% | 10% | 100% | 30% |
| Understand Customer Needs | 10% | Product intro responses on-site (#) | 50% | 5% | 80 | 100 | 125% | 6% |
| | | Follow-up information requested from PM (#) | 50% | 5% | 40 | 70 | 175% | 9% |
| Grow Event | 10% | Year-over-year growth (%) | 100% | 10% | 5% | 4% | 80% | 8% |

## Conclusion

Tradeshows and events are a big investment. Companies need to make sure they are getting a return on their event-marketing investment. Measuring event ROI is critical to the understanding of what marketing tools are most effective for your organization. Event measurement, while modestly complex, need not be difficult. If cross-functional teams agree to measurable objectives and metrics, event elements and content can be focused on achieving the desired results and providing the greatest return, and reduction, or even elimination, of spending on those event elements or content that don't provide a return. Event measurement enables management to evaluate events vs. other marketing and investment opportunities.

## CASE STUDY
## A Practical Study in Using VOC Data to
## Determine Event ROI

**The Event.** Distributor convention.

**The Challenge.** A major malted-beverage manufacturer holds annual meetings to kick off its selling season and to deploy sales and marketing plans for the next twelve months. The event was becoming stale as elements were being produced because they had "always done it that way." The challenge was to revitalize the event by making content more relevant to the audience while demonstrating measurable return-on-investment to senior management.

**The Objective.** MM Company wants to make the convention a transformational experience by creating a powerful impact on people's feelings, opinions, intentions, abilities, perceptions and behaviors when it really counts — after the meeting, in the marketplace. It also wants to deliver measurable ROI.

**The Solution.** Previously, MM Company produced a "speaker-driven" event instead of a "customer-responsive" event. As a result of this thinking, the convention was fatally flawed from the beginning and could not fulfill its potential to move attendees toward new feelings, perceptions and behaviors. Pre- and post-event audience surveys provided MM Company with a very clear picture of what was necessary to build a highly relevant meeting for attendees and measure ROI for the organization. The process consisted of five components:

1. Pre-meeting VOC qualitative research identified attendees' interests, business concerns, issues, needs, desires, suggestions and preferences for the meeting.
2. Pre-meeting quantitative research confirmed and refined learnings and provided a baseline for measurement of ROI.
3. Most importantly, the meeting design and event plan utilized research findings to develop measurable objectives and meeting strategies.
4. The event was produced using the meeting design and event plan as a guideline. Additional networking sessions were added and the overall event was shortened by eliminating non-needed elements and non-relevant content. Additional resources were added to make content as sharp and concise as possible.
5. Post-meeting quantitative research measured attendees' positive satisfaction levels and positive shifts in their attitudes, perceptions, intentions and behaviors.
6. Return-On-Event was calculated by comparing findings on pre- and post-meeting benchmark questions.

**The Results.** The major malted-beverage manufacturer was able to target its resources to achieve maximum attendee impact while eliminating extraneous (and expensive) meeting elements. MM Company now knows exactly how well its meeting performed. It knows precisely what results it produces and what specific actions it needs to take to reinforce strengths and address areas of weakness when planning future conventions. Overall, the VOC process represented about three percent of the company's total meeting investment.

**Barry Seidenstat**, PMP, is a project management professional with over 26 years of broad experience in brand marketing communications; event management and production; channel marketing and communications; brand management; and database lead generation management. He successfully uses his six-sigma quality certification and its VOC process in all communications he produces. He has had a variety of marketing communications positions with Coors Brewing Company and General Electric. Currently, he is the owner of ROI Communications Solutions, an event-marketing agency specializing in assisting companies develop and prove their event ROI. Barry joined BMA Colorado in 1999.

## About the Business Marketing Association (BMA)

Originally founded in 1922 as the National Industrial Advertising Association, today's Business Marketing Association focuses solely on the field of business-to-business (B2B) marketing. BMA provides a wide range of services, resources, and opportunities to help meet the daily challenges of sustaining business profitability and enhancing the development of B2B marketing professionals.

BMA Colorado is the region's premier association for B2B marketing practitioners. A 13-time national BMA Chapter of the Year award winner, member benefits include expert speakers on innovative industry topics, unparalleled networking with more than 400 members, professional recognition and a vast library of educational materials.

## How To Order Additional Books

Additional copies of *Advice From the Top: The Expert Guide to B2B Marketing* are available through BMA Colorado. Special discounts are available for BMA members, accredited colleges and universities, and for bulk orders of 50 books or more. For more information, or to order additional books, please write to book@bmacolorado.org or call the BMA Colorado office at 303-607-9957.